THE LAST DAYS OF
SITTING BULL
SIOUX MEDICINE CHIEF

SITTING BULL AND "BUFFALO BILL"
IN BUFFALO BILL'S WILD WEST SHOW

THE LAST DAYS OF
SITTING BULL
SIOUX MEDICINE CHIEF

Usher L. Burdick

COACHWHIP PUBLICATIONS

Landisville, Pennsylvania

The Last Days of Sitting Bull, by Usher L. Burdick
Copyright © 2011 Coachwhip Publications
No claim made on public domain material.

First published 1941

ISBN 1-61646-100-4
ISBN-13 978-1-61646-100-3

Front Cover Image: Sitting Bull, by Palmquist & Jurgens (1884)
Back Cover Image: Sitting Bull and his nephew, One Bull, by Palmquist &
    Jurgens (1884)

CoachwhipBooks.com

CONTENTS

Dedicated to my Sioux Friends in North and South Dakota, who are the descendants of the great Sioux tribes who fought a losing battle in the protection of their homes.

INTRODUCTION

Among the valuable papers and documents, relating to the Sioux, left among the effects of the late Major James McLaughlin, agent and inspector among the Sioux for a half century, was a complete collection of letters, telegrams, and army documents, telling the exact story of the attempted capture and death of Sitting Bull on Grand River, December 15, 1890. These papers and documents came into my possession through the courtesy of Major Mc-Laughlin's daughter-in-law, Mrs. R. S. McLaughlin of McLaughlin, South Dakota. Those papers and documents are published in the Appendix of this volume. Since these letters and telegrams were official communications exchanged between Major McLaughlin, as Indian Agent at Fort Yates, and the Interior Department and the War Department, the proof of this story is as complete as the facts of history can be written.

It has been necessary to supply facts, data and material from other sources too, in order to present an unbiased narrative of the Last Days of Sitting Bull. Probably no other incident in the history of the West has precipitated as many stories, articles and books as the subject here treated. All of the publicity during his lifetime and after his death has, no doubt, made the name "Sitting Bull" known to more people now living than any other Indian of the Sioux Nation.

His greatness as an Indian warrior, viewed from the standpoint of Indians and White, has been eclipsed by many other Sioux. None of the others, however, did things in such a spectacular way as Sitting Bull. He gained nation-wide and even an international reputation, while traveling in America and Europe with Buffalo Bill. His pictures, life size, were pasted on buildings, fences, and billboards in America and Europe. Touring the country with such a master showman as Buffalo Bill brought his name to the attention of millions. Making this grand circuit, as he did, starting in 1885, just nine years after the annihilation of General Custer and his command, undoubtedly made a deep and lasting impression on people everywhere.

Those who know the Indians will hardly be heard to say that as a warrior he was the equal of Crow King, Gall, Two Moons, or Crazy Horse, his contemporaries. As a warrior among them, he was all but forgotten. What Indian has said he engaged in battle on the day of Custer's death? Yet, many stories have been written, telling of Sitting Bull, the great Sioux warrior.

He was cunning, canny, well-informed for an Indian, and an implacable enemy of the White people. He resented the treatment his people had received from the Government. He had seen treaties made by the Government and broken without provocation. He saw the oncoming tide of civilization that pushed the Sioux farther Westward year by year. He was an Indian, yet well enough informed to know that eventually the Indian must be driven from his home, unless determined resistance were offered by the Indian himself.

He knew there was no chance in an open fight, hence, to his mind, any means to check the coming of settlers was justified. He used the powers with which he was gifted, not those of a warrior, but those of a preacher. In that capacity he fought for his people, and in that capacity he died. His surrender was characteristic of him; at first he offered no resistance whatever. Would inaction have been the policy taken by a Gall or a Crazy Horse?

He was powerful as a preacher. He gathered his people around him on every possible occasion and exhorted them to protect their lands. He talked to them, he held out to his followers the vision of a lost people to be supplanted soon by the Whites. He coaxed his people and ordered them to resist. In the final chapter of his life, when ordinary preaching would not arouse his people, he resorted to the mysteries of the Ghost Dance to arouse their waning interest in fighting for their lands.

In this, no Indian deserves more credit. He did more to arouse his people to fight for their own homes than any other Indian among all the tribes of the Sioux. When argument failed, he used the promise of the Great Messiah to rid the land of the Whites, destroy their Power, bring back the dead Indians and the buffalo, and make a Happy Hunting Ground of their fast disappearing homes. Whether he believed the story or not makes little difference, as apparently nothing else could have stirred his followers. This plan worked. His followers were stirred, yet the futility of their resistance must have been known to him. He converted very few of his own people, and he met his greatest resistance among them. The great warrior, Gall, took no part in the dances. Rain-In-The-Face offered to arrest him, and bring him back to the fort, if the Government would furnish guns and permit the opportunity.

Sitting Bull had always been a dealer in "Medicine." He would come often to the councils with some plan of action that he had interpreted from his "Medicine." The Ghost Dance was purely Indian "Medicine." How anyone can say he was not a "Medicine Man," when he died in the midst of it, is difficult to explain.

Knowing the Indians well, there cannot be the slightest reason to detract from the greatness of this chief. He made his last stand and, perhaps to his mind, the only stand that was possible for any Indian to make, to resist the onrush of the tide of Whites to occupy the land of his forefathers. It must be said, however, that he was never a great warrior in any period of his life.

An account of the "Messiah Craze" will be presented in full followed in the Appendix, by the actual documents of the events pertaining to the trouble.

This narrative is intended to be as near to the actual facts of the matter, as it will ever be possible to record it. It remains for each reader to make his own estimate of Sitting Bull.

Writers in the past have relied altogether too much on interviews with only a few of the Indians who were associated with the great chief. The survivors of those men and women are now very old, and, like the Whites, they do not readily recall facts and events which occurred over forty years ago. In the summer of 1931, the writer had interviews with sixty-two of the aging followers. This narrative presents therefrom a great drama of Indian History as it was probably staged.

In any event, it is hoped this story will be of some historical value to the present generation and to the future generations who will inhabit the land of the Sioux.

USHER L. BURDICK.

Williston, North Dakota,
February 21, 1941.

I

A SKETCH OF THE LIFE OF SITTING BULL

Sitting Bull[1] (Tatanka Iyotanka), son of Four Horns, a sub-chief of the Sioux, was born in the year 1834 on the Grand River in Dakota Territory (now a part of South Dakota).

At the age of fourteen he accompanied his father in a war party against the Crows and here it was that he counted his first coup (touching with his stick the dead body of the enemy). On their return the father was very proud of his young son and gave a great feast and announced that his son should henceforth be known as "Four Horn." In the Winter Count of the Sioux (Pictographic History) Sitting Bull is recorded as Four Horn. He was given the name of Sitting Bull early in his life in accordance with the true Indian custom, and, as he grew in power among his people, he preferred the name of Sitting Bull to his father's name of Four Horn.

From the time of counting his first "coup" he joined in repeated war parties against the Shoshone and the Crows. In 1868 he instigated an assault against Fort Buford, a Dakota Territory, which resulted in the destruction of the saw mill there. He carried away the circular saw which he used as a musical instrument by suspending it and beating the sides with a steel hammer. When thus struck, this saw produced a weird ring that fit exactly in war dance music, and had a tendency to step up the dance to a higher pitch than could be done by the old fashioned tom-tom.

Most of the excursions in which Sitting Bull took part, from his early youth up to the time of the Custer Battle, had been war parties or horse-stealing raids against their natural enemies. To

11

the old Sioux no higher honors could be bestowed on any Indian than that of "stealing" horses from his enemies.

White Bull, a nephew of Sitting Bull, in his pictographic record of the Custer Battle, adds a few chapters to the peroration of his life in pictures which portray him "stealing horses" from his enemies and driving them back to the Sioux camp. No Indian could be a coward and be a successful "horse stealer." It took nerve and courage and Sitting Bull possessed both qualities in a high degree. To say that he was a "medicine man" and not a warrior, is a true statement concerning his later life, but that statement does not mean that he did not have courage and the daring possessed by actual warriors.

One of the best accounts ever written about Sitting Bull's actual status among his own people can be found in A. McG. Beede's book, *Sitting Bull's Custer*. Mr. Beede was a highly educated Protestant Missionary who located at Fort Yates, North Dakota. He lived many years among the Sioux and knew them intimately.

Among other things Mr. Beede says, "Sitting Bull was a rebel to the last. He was harassed and hounded, but never crushed. He had hopes of a Dakota nationality when everything human pointed to its impossibility. He believed he was divinely appointed to bring about this desirable end. He was neither a child nor a fool and realized the odds against him. He was not a warrior but an Indian prophet. All he wanted was to be let alone. He wanted peace, but fought that he might have it.

"He was too intensely patriotic to allow his people to submit themselves to the White man's ways. He was a friend of little children, women and old people. He enforced justice and whenever his hunters came back to camp loaded down with the choice meat of the prairies, it was first distributed to the aged and crippled and the needy, all of them adored Sitting Bull." . . .

"Expediency never took the place of his belief, although his belief must inevitably lead to a clash and the subjugation of his people in the end. He never made war on White man's land, but fought in his own country to preserve it for the Indians. The army was a tool of robbing the Indians of his ancestral lands and turning them over to stockmen and farmers. This sturdy old heathen clung to the policy of his forefathers till a bullet put him to sleep. Sitting Bull was a teetotaler."

Sitting Bull was always serious and never joked. He was magnanimous with his enemies and never killed a captive.

His life's work of building a strong Indian nationality took him into contact with many tribes. He made friends with the Nez Perce of Idaho, the Assiniboines of Montana and the Cheyennes to the South. He made friends with the Utes of Oregon and with the Crees of Canada. He made war upon the Crows because they would not federate with him in building a strong Indian nation to fight the White man's horde of settlers who were taking, each day, some new part of the Indian domain. Sitting Bull knew that when the land was settled that the buffalo and the antelope would disappear and since these animals supplied every want of the Indian, it was highly important to protect this food supply. Sitting Bull never wanted anything for himself, but he always, in his speeches, referred to his children who would come after him.

He was a great orator, and while a Hunkpapa himself, he was recognized as a great "Medicine Man" among all the Sioux and the Cheyennes. Sitting Bull cannot be given credit for being the greatest orator, for Major McLaughlin and David F. Barry, who are considered authorities on the subject, assert that Chief Running Antelope was the greatest orator of the Sioux Nation and that John Grass (Jumping Bear) had a similar reputation. While not possessing the natural power of Chief Running Antelope, yet his wonderful memory gave to John Grass his great fame as an orator.[2]

After the Custer Battle, Sitting Bull escaped to Canada and for five years wandered with his people, a fugitive from justice. When he surrendered at Fort Buford, Dakota Territory, in July, 1881, he was the last Chief of the Sioux to lay down his arms. Gall, Crow King, Crazy Horse, and Two Moons, all had given up the unequal fight before the implacable "Medicine Man," the arch enemy of the Whites, consented to leave the War Path. He was never conquered

Sitting Bull's Contract with Buffalo
Bill's Wild West Show.

Standing Rock Agency, D. T.
This Agreement entered into this sixth
day of June, 1885. between John M.
Burke General Manager of the "Buffalo
Bill Wild West Show", and Sitting
Bull and party consisting of ten peoples.
I, John M. Burke do hereby agree
to pay Sitting Bull Fifty ($50.00)
Dollars per week, to be paid weekly
every Saturday night,— Five (5)
Indians at Twenty five ($25.00)
Dollars per month each, paid monthly;
Three Indian women at Fifteen ($15.00)
Dollars per month Each, to be paid
monthly; and William Halsey
Interpreter to be paid Sixty ($60.00)
Dollars per month, also to be paid
monthly. It is also agreed that
Sitting Bull is also to receive One
hundred and Twenty five Dollars as
a present, and the first two weeks
pay in advance, being a total

of Five Hundred and Twenty five ($225.⁰⁰) Dollars before leaving his home at Standing Rock Agency. D.T. The receipt of which is hereby acknowledged.

Sitting Bull and party do hereby agree to travel with the "Buffalo Bill Wild West Show" in consideration of the above named remunerations, for their services rendered during the exhibitions of the aforesaid Show, and under Continuous control of said management. for summer season of four months. (1885) and if extended to be at same terms.

John M. Burke does also agree to pay all expenses of the party from Standing Rock, to the Show. and to pay all expenses of the party from the Show to Standing Rock at expiration of this Contract.

James McLaughlin
Standing Rock Agency
Joseph Primeau
Standing Rock agency

Witnesses

John M. Burke
Bus. Manager Cody & Salsbury

Sitting Bull

P.S. Sitting Bull is to have sole right to sell his own Photographs and Autographs.
John M. Burke
Bus. Manager Cody & Salsbury

and he never quit preaching against the Whites. His last uprising was a religious one. His whole religion and his whole soul was set against the Whites. He was a savage preacher to a savage people, and therein lay his power. His final act on earth, that of starting armed resistance against the Indian police, was not so much an act of personal bravery as it was an effort to retain his power with his followers who believed in him. At first he offered to surrender peacefully, but being twitted by his young son, who pronounced him a coward in the presence of his followers, was too much for the great preacher—then it was that he fought, dying as he had preached.[3]

Sitting Bull was a small man, bowlegged and keen-eyed, nothing escaped his attention. His nose was large indicating leadership. In talking to Whites he was always on his guard, and regarded all movements of his White friends with suspicion. With his own people he was generous, just, and never lost an opportunity to impress his hearers with the idea that they all owed a duty to their children—that of preserving the Indian lands for the peace and enjoyment in the years to come. He had plenty of imagination, and could see far ahead of his day.

He married two sisters who lived with him until his death, each bearing him children, and all lived together in perfect harmony. He has one son still living, but his only other son, Crow Foot, was killed with his father on Grand River. Many Indians have tried to pass themselves off as sons of Sitting Bull, but never succeeded in establishing any blood connection. His daughters married in the Grand River country and many of his grandchildren still live in the valley of the Grand River. He left two noted nephews, who accompanied the old chief in all events leading up to the Custer Battle, and his subsequent surrender at Fort Buford. Those two are White Bull, in Cherry Creek, South Dakota, and One Bull at Little Eagle, South Dakota.

After the return of Sitting Bull from Fort Randall in 1883, there was peace and quiet on the reservation until the Act of Congress passed in 1889. During these years Sitting Bull was in Buffalo Bill's

Wild West show from 1885 to 1887. He frequently visited the Agency and talked matters over with Major McLaughlin. Buffalo Bill traveled across the United States, showed in England, France and Spain. The longer the show lasted the more widespread this reputation of Sitting Bull grew.

Sitting Bull received $50.00 per week and was privileged to sell moccasins and other trinkets made by his wives and friends. He would autograph his name on a card for $1.00, and he also autographed moccasins. When he ran out of moccasins more were forwarded from the Reservation, and at one time there were more pairs of Sitting Bull's moccasins in the hands of trophy and relic hunters than there were Indians with him at the time of this surrender.

Sitting Bull could sign his name well, but he could write nothing else. His penmanship was faultless. Since it is known how he learned to sign his name, it might be well to relate it here. Gus Hedderich, a member of the firm of Leighton, Jordan and Hedderich, traders at Fort Buford, Poplar, and Woody Mountain, Canada, was an expert accountant and penman. While Sitting Bull was a fugitive in Canada, he traded at Woody Mountain, and became an intimate friend of Gus Hedderich. During the winter months the old chief spent much time at the trading post. Hedderich showed him how to write "Sitting Bull," and Sitting Bull not only learned to write that name but to do it in the penmanship style of Hedderich.

A heated controversy has arisen over the question of whether Sitting Bull took part in the Custer Battle. From nearly countless interviews with the Indians who participated in it, the Author learned that Sitting Bull did not do any actual shooting, and took no part other than assisting in rounding up the pony herd and moving the women and children out of harm's way of the actual battle. Perhaps the best authority on what Sitting Bull did on this occasion would be Sitting Bull himself. While he was in Canada in 1879 and peace commissioners from the United States were trying to induce him to return, his speech to them was taken in short hand

and transcribed by the reporter. In that statement Sitting Bull substantiates what has been related to the Author regarding the actual battle.[4]

On one occasion the Major told the chief that since he was married to two women, he would have to get rid of one, as he had promised to live like the White man, with one wife. Sitting Bull said that he could not do that because he liked both of his wives and would not know which one to give up. The Major called his attention to the fact that Sitting Bull had agreed to live the ways of a White man, and said, "Didn't you agree to live like a White man?" "Yes," said Sitting Bull, "I agreed to do that, and I will do it. I will live just like a White man: you give me a White wife and you can have both my Indian wives." This was said with a twinkle in his eye and with a slight grin of sarcasm, which left the Major without much further to say. At any rate, Sitting Bull kept his wives and they were with him when he met his death.

Following the fight at Grand River, Sitting Bull's name became very unpopular among the Indians themselves. There were a great many women and children made widows and orphans because of Sitting Bull's action. At the scene of the battle, the Indian police were under the orders of Lieutenant Bull Head, but after he fell, mortally wounded, Red Tomahawk assumed command. Red Tomahawk ordered the body of Sitting Bull placed in a wagon, along with the bodies of the dead policemen. This order the Indian police refused to obey, as they said they did not want their friends to have to ride in the wagon with this man. After some urging by Red Tomahawk, the policemen agreed to put Sitting Bull's body in the wagon, and then piled the bodies of the policemen on top of it. This was done and in that condition, the wagon, carrying the dead, arrived at Fort Yates.

The body of Sitting Bull was buried without Christian rites, just outside of the old military post burial grounds at Fort Yates. At the time of his death, neither Indian nor White man would honor him with a decent burial. All other bodies have been removed from the grounds, and Sitting Bull reigns there supreme. A few years ago a cement top and proper marker was placed on his grave by friends.

In later years, this feeling against the name of Sitting Bull was mellowed, and even went beyond that; he is looked upon by not a few Indians as a great dreamer—dreaming for the best interests of the Indians—and they are sorry now that they did not follow his advice. Among many he now occupies a position of Saint.

In view of the open and notorious violations by the Government of Indian Treaties, we cannot defend the charge made by Sitting Bull that all bald-headed White men were liars, and that all agents of the Government sent out to obtain treaty ratifications were bald-headed.

When William F. Cody, better known as Buffalo Bill, organized his Wild West Show, like P. T. Barnum, he wanted to give the people what they wanted. Buffalo Bill was a showman. He conceived the idea that the public, both at home and abroad, would like to see the Sioux Chief who wiped out the Custer Command. After obtaining special authority from the War Department, Sitting Bull made a contract with John M. Burke, manager for Buffalo Bill, by which the Great Chief and his party of Indians agreed to appear with the Wild West Show. Burke understood the art of advertising and realized its value. One of the first pieces of advertisement published was a life-size picture of Sitting Bull in full war regalia and representing him to be the great Sioux Warrior who had massacred the Custer Command.

FOOTNOTES

[1] See White Bull's *Pictographic History of the Custer Battle*.
[2] See *Indian Notes on Custer Battle*, by D. F. Barry—*My Friend The Indian*, by Maj. James McLaughlin.
[3] See *Story of Fort Buford*, by Usher L. Burdick.
[4] *Horrors of Indian Warfare*, by Halloway, St. Louis, 1891.

DAVID F. BARRY, NOTED INDIAN PHOTOGRAPHER, AND
MAJOR JAMES McLAUGHLIN

II

A SKETCH OF THE LIFE OF MAJOR JAMES MCLAUGHLIN

James McLaughlin[1] was born at Avonmore, Ontario, Canada, February 12, 1842. He was educated in the common school at that place and came west in 1853, locating at Wabasha, Minnesota, where he later was engaged in the trade of a blacksmith. In 1864 he married Marie L. Buisson (pronounced Besaw) of Wabasha. Marie L. Buisson was a quarter-bred Sioux, being the granddaughter of Ha-za-ho-ta-win, a pure bred Sioux woman who was reported to have been a striking beauty in her day.

The autobiography of Marie McLaughlin says: "In publishing these 'Myths of the Sioux,' I deem it proper to state that I am of one-fourth Sioux blood. My maternal grandfather, Captain Duncan Graham, a Scotchman by birth, who had seen service in the British Army, was one of a party of Scotch Highlanders who, in 1811, arrived in the British Northwest by way of York Factory, Hudson Bay, to found what was known as the Selkirk Colony, near Lake Winnipeg, now within the province of Manitoba, Canada. Soon after his arrival at Lake Winnipeg, he proceeded up the Red River of the North and the western fork thereof, to its source, and thence down the Minnesota River to Mendota, the confluence of the Minnesota and Mississippi Rivers, where he located. My grandmother, Ha-za-ho-ta-win, was a full-blood of the Medawakanton Band of the Sioux Tribe of Indians. My father, Joseph Buisson, born near Montreal, Canada, was connected with the American Fur Company, with headquarters at Mendota, Minnesota, which point was for

21

many years the chief distributing depot of the American Fur Company, from which the Indian trade conducted by that company on the upper Mississippi was directed.

"I was born December 8, 1842, at Wabasha, Minnesota, then Indian country, and resided there until fourteen years of age, when I was sent to school at Prairie du Chien, Wisconsin.

"I was married to Major James McLaughlin at Mendota, Minnesota, January 28, 1864, and resided in Minnesota until July 1, 1871, when I accompanied my husband to Devils Lake Agency, North Dakota, then Dakota Territory, where I remained ten years in most friendly relations with the Indians of that Agency. My husband was Indian agent at Devils Lake Agency, and in 1881, was transferred to Standing Rock, on the Missouri River, then a very important agency, to take charge of the Sioux who had then but recently surrendered to the military authorities, and been brought by steamboat from various points on the upper Missouri, to be permanently located on the Standing Rock Reservation.

"Having been born and reared in an Indian community, I, at an early age, acquired a thorough knowledge of the Sioux language, and having lived on Indian reservations for the past forty years in a position which brought me very near the Indians, whose confidence I possessed, I have, therefore, had exceptional opportunities of learning the legends and folk-lore of the Sioux."

On July 1, 1871, James McLaughlin and his wife moved to Fort Totten, Dakota Territory, where he became Agency blacksmith. He soon picked up the Sioux language and became a great friend of the Indians. His work among them was soon recognized, for on June 10, 1876, he was appointed Agent of Fort Totten Indian Reservation by President U. S. Grant, and reappointed by President R. B. Hayes, June 14, 1880.

In the early spring of 1881, General William T. Sherman made a tour of the western forts and knowing that the wild bands of the Sioux, held prisoners at Fort Buford, would soon be rounded up and taken back to Standing Rock Indian Reservation, at Fort Yates, he insisted that Major McLaughlin be sent there as agent. He personally requested Major McLaughlin to accept the post. Accordingly, on June 29, 1881, the Major resigned as Agent at Fort Totten. His resignation was accepted on July 29, 1881.

Joseph A. Stephan was agent at Standing Rock at the time of McLaughlin's appointment and resigned to facilitate the change. For the balance of Stephan's term, President James A. Garfield issued the appointment dated June 27, 1881. On October 27, 1881, President Chester A. Arthur issued his regular appointment of McLaughlin as Agent at Standing Rock for a four year term. Again, on October 14, 1885, McLaughlin was appointed agent at Standing Rock by President Cleveland, the same being a recess appointment. On April 24, 1886, President Cleveland issued his regular appointment for a full four year term. Again on April 15, 1890, President Benjamin Harrison appointed him agent at Standing Rock for a four year term. On May 9, 1894, during his second term, President Cleveland reappointed McLaughlin agent at Standing Rock for another period of four years.

Many agreements and the ratification of Acts of Congress were being submitted to the Indians in the various parts of the United States, and with his service of twenty-four years among the Indians, Major McLaughlin became the logical man for the position, and, accordingly, on January 19, 1895, he was appointed to the post of Indian Inspector, by President Grover Cleveland. To this post he was reappointed by President William McKinley on February 14, 1899. On January 19, 1903, he was reappointed to the same post by President Theodore Roosevelt, and again on January 19, 1907, reappointed by President Theodore Roosevelt.

In addition to the appointments named above, he was reappointed as Indian Inspector by President Taft, and President Woodrow Wilson. He died in active service on July 28, 1923, at the age of 81 years. While his death occurred in the city of Washington, he was buried in South Dakota, in the town that bears his name.

There were the following children born to Mary L. and Major McLaughlin: John, Melda, Harry, Charles and Sibley, all of whom are now dead. The grandchildren and great-grandchildren now number thirty-nine.

Major McLaughlin abolished the cruel Sioux Sun Dance while he was in the service at Fort Totten.

He was personally and intimately acquainted with all the great Indian Chiefs of the United States, and was author of the book entitled, *My Friend the Indian*, which is considered today the most accurate of the Sioux Tribes. *Myths of the Sioux*, was written and published by his wife, Mary L. (Marie), and is illustrated with genuine Sioux drawings and is one of the unique Sioux books in existence.

Mrs. McLaughlin died on August 5, 1924, and lies buried beside her husband in the Catholic cemetery at McLaughlin, South Dakota. As long as there are Sioux Indians or their descendants, the names of Mary and Major McLaughlin will be a part of the Sioux history. No man ever lived who knew the Sioux better.

It should be remembered that during all of Major McLaughlin's life and service among the Sioux, he was an employee of the Indian Bureau and naturally conformed to the orders of that department. Had he been free to act at all times as his own knowledge and understanding dictated, he would have been of greater value to the Indians and the Government. Being, as he was, an employee of the Bureau, he did not always have his own way nor could he question the policy of the Indian Bureau and the Department of the Interior.

His long record of service, with almost a score of Indian Commissioners and Secretaries of the Interior, is unquestioned evidence that at all times he acted within the orders of these Departments of the Government.

His letter files are replete with letters to his superior officers, giving detailed facts concerning difficult matters and giving his conclusions as to what should be done, but once having received his orders, he carried them out with the exactness of military discipline.

The Indian Bureau has always been a detriment to the American Indians. It is responsible for the mis-use of millions of dollars of Indian Trust funds. It has always advocated the enslavement of the American Indian. While Congress has always been the responsible party in the Government's dealings with the Indians, yet the worst thing which can be said about Congress or any member of it is that it has blindly followed the advice of the Department of the Interior and the Indian Bureau. I know of no case where Congress or any Member of it purposely and intentionally was a party to defrauding Indians, but in following the Department of the Interior and the Indian Bureau, the action of Congress, time and time again, has resulted in depriving the American Indians of their just dues.

Being so closely allied with the Indian Bureau for so many years, it is naturally to be expected that Major McLaughlin was not without his critics. Carefully analyzed, the criticism leveled against him in his lifetime, and now frequently mentioned by many writers of Sioux History, can be said to be a criticism of the Indian Bureau, not personally chargeable to Major McLaughlin.

During all of his long service among the Sioux, he never broke a promise to the Indians, and labored diligently and honestly for the best interests of the Sioux, under many handicaps of the Indian Bureau.

FOOTNOTES
[1] See *Myths of the Sioux*, by Marie McLaughlin.

THE OLD INDIANS IN THIS PHOTOGRAPH WERE FOLLOWERS OF SITTING BULL OR POLICEMEN DURING

THE GHOST DANCE TROUBLE

III

WAS MCLAUGHLIN PREJUDICED?

Many reports, some in book form, state that there was an unfriendly feeling between Sitting Bull and Major McLaughlin. There have been some reports published asserting this difference between the two was due to religious differences, Major McLaughlin being a Catholic and Sitting Bull a Protestant. These reports are not sustained by any competent evidence. In the first place, Major McLaughlin always had the support of Protestant missionaries, just as strongly as he had the support of Catholic missionaries. Secondly, while Sitting Bull was reported to be a Protestant, he was, nevertheless, an Indian and believed in the Indian religion of his fathers with more dependence and assurance of the hereafter than he did in the religion of either the Catholic or Protestant denominations. In the next place, at the time of this trouble, Sitting Bull was a preacher of the Messiah Craze, which was Indian. To claim he was a Protestant must be to say that the Messiah Craze was a form of Protestant religion. It was not—it was not Catholic—it was Indian.

Finally, Sitting Bull was against anything that was "White." He was a foe to everything that was White, and the last thing on earth that he would embrace as his religion would be the White man's religion, whether Protestant or Catholic. Many zealous missionaries, in the early years of their work, would feel amply repaid for their hardship and privations by having the Indian embrace their chosen faith, only to realize when death approached, these same converts would resort to the Old Indian Religion, and would rather

27

die in the hope of being transferred to the Happy Hunting Ground, where there were no white men, than to have faith in the hereafter as preached by the faithful missionaries.

There was no trouble between the two until the Act of Congress[1] opening up the Reservation for settlement was brought to the Indians for their approval or rejection. McLaughlin, being Agency Superintendent, and entirely subservient to the Indian Bureau, urged the Indians to vote for the Act. Sitting Bull, who could see the end of Indian independence, opposed the Act. In this contest the Indian Bureau was too strong for Sitting Bull to prevail. All the power of the Federal Government, all Indian Officers and employees, were massed then as they are today, on the side of the Indian Bureau. Every employee, then as now, must support and advocate what the Indian Bureau prescribes.

This contest resulted in strained relations between Major McLaughlin and Sitting Bull. Seeing himself a loser in the fight to prevent ratification, and seeing his own people desert him and line up with the Government, there is not much wonder that Sitting Bull became insolent and refused to obey any Government regulation. He instituted the "Ghost Dance" on Grand River in violation of Agency orders; he refused to come into the Agency upon orders from the Superintendent. The fact, of course, is that as the "Ghost Dance" increased, so did the number of followers of Sitting Bull in his fight to ignore the Act of Congress opening up the Reservation for settlement.

Prior to this time, the relations between the Major and Sitting Bull had been most friendly. After having been agent at Fort Totten, Dakota Territory, Major McLaughlin came to Fort Yates as agent in 1881. At that time, Sitting Bull was a fugitive from justice, roaming the plains of Montana, Dakota and Canada. He did not surrender until July 19, 1881. After his surrender, he was held a prisoner with all his followers at Fort Buford, Dakota Territory, until steamboats were secured to transport them down the river. On the first trip down river in the summer of 1881, Sitting Bull, together with 150 immediate followers, was transported to Fort Randall, where they were held prisoners of war until the spring of 1883.

While at Fort Randall, Sitting Bull appealed to McLaughlin to intercede for him, and permit him and his followers to return to Grand River and live in peace with the Whites, under the direction of the Government. McLaughlin did intercede; it was McLaughlin who was responsible for the permission of the Government to the Hunkpapas for their return to their native homes on Grand River.

It was only through the influence of McLaughlin that the Government in 1885 permitted Sitting Bull to tour America and Europe with Buffalo Bill.[2]

From all the evidence presented here, it seems established beyond any reasonable doubt, that there was no religious prejudice in the mind of Major McLaughlin, in any of his dealings with Sitting Bull.

Probably the best contemporary opinion to be formed of the situation leading up to the death of Sitting Bull can be gained from letters written at the time by Major McLaughlin to his friends, copies of which letters are still legible in his copy book of letters which the Author has. All of these letters were written in long hand and were pressed in a copy book with a moistened cloth in the usual way of preserving a copy in the early days.

In a letter written to Herbert Welsh, Philadelphia, Pa., dated at Standing Rock, November 25, 1890, the Major says:

> "My Dear Mr. Welsh:
>
> "I have the honor to acknowledge your letter of inquiry on the 19th inst and in reply would state that the Messiah Craze has assumed serious proportions among the Sioux, but it is confined chiefly to the non-progressive and those who refused to ratify the Act of March 2nd, 1889, and are taking advantage of the craze to organize opposition to recognizing the validity of the Act.
>
> "The 'Ghost Dance' as practiced among the Sitting Bull faction here, which is doubtless the same as that practiced among the other Sioux, is most pernicious and the demoralizing effect can only be fully understood by witnessing one of the dances. It is wonderful to see how

zealous the ordinary Indians are in their faith of this false
Christ, their credulity and inherent superstition making
them an easy prey to the more wily prophets and cunning
impostors of Medicine Men, while the Chief Priests seem
to succeed in deceiving themselves as well as each other
in their misleading nonsense and extending the foolish
craze, and while there are but few Indians brave enough
to express themselves as not believing in the new doctrine.
I have, however, succeeded in keeping it from getting a
foothold in any of the camps outside of the Grand River
settlements and were it not for Sitting Bull who was
encouraged by numerous gifts and illy advised during
the past year by a Mrs. C. Weldon of Brooklyn, N. Y.,
who visited here claiming to be a member of Dr. Bland's
Indian Defense Association and much like the latter, the
absurd doctrine would never have been practiced openly
at this Agency, and even now, if allowed to carry out
my plans, it will be suppressed without military aid or
bloodshed.

"The weather thus far is so mild and summer-like that
it is unfavorable for any attempt at breaking into the powers of the Medicine Men, as Sitting Bull announced some
weeks ago that he would not have any snow fall or cold
weather experienced this winter, so that the Ghost Dance
could be continued without discomfort until the Messiah
appeared among them next spring, and I am, therefore,
waiting for a cold spell to set in before expecting a sufficient change in their ardor so as to justify my attacking
their false worship in a tangible form by withholding
rations from all those participating

"Sitting Bull is a lover of disturbance and mischief
making, who clings to the old Indian ways and is an
active opponent to civilization, therefore, he, with a few
others of the disaffected leaders whose presence among
these people is baneful, should be removed from the Sioux
country.

"While the religious craze has a serious aspect at present I am confident that if prudence is used in handling it and nothing done to precipitate a conflict until the weather turns colder, the excitement will die out so that the Indians can be met and talked to and when their reason is restored, they certainly can be convinced of the absurdity of this foolish doctrine into which they have been led by a few cunning impostors who wish to regain their former prestige among their people and notoriety in the public press.

"I am, Sir, Very respectfully

"Your Obedient Serv't,

"James McLaughlin,

"*U. S. Indian Agent.*"

No better evidence of the kindly feeling the Major had for Sitting Bull at all times could be produced than the letter written to Sitting Bull by Major McLaughlin December thirteenth, just two days before Sitting Bull was killed on Grand River. This letter was carried and delivered to Sitting Bull on the fourteenth by One Bull (Tatankawanazi), a nephew of Sitting Bull. This letter was copied by the old press method and is in the long hand of Major McLaughlin. It reads:

"Standing Rock,

December 13, 1890.

"Friend Sitting Bull

"I have just received your letter sent in by Tatankawanazi (One Bull) and as you know that I have been, and am, a good friend to the Sioux and anxious to see them prosperous and happy you should listen to my advice. I have always been your friend. I got you released from prison when you were confined at Fort Randall and I saved you: from going into the guard house when General Logan and the other two Senators were here in August, 1883. I also overlooked many mistakes and offenses of yours and if you think deep in your heart you will surely feel that I have been a true friend and gave you good advice at all times, and that no bad ever followed when you did as I advised; and that by listening to my advice yourself and people have houses, stoves, bedsteads, chairs, wagons, teams and many things that the poorer white people do not possess. The Government is the best friend to the Indians and they should do what is pleasing to the 'Great Father' who knows what they most need and directs them in the ways they should go. It makes me happy to see the Indians under my care obedient to the 'Great Father,' trying to better their condition, and it makes my heart sad when any of them act unwise and do anything harmful to them as individuals or as a people. The Ghost Dance that some are now engaged in is hurtful in many respects, no good can come from it and if not soon discontinued bad results will certainly follow.

"The over-credulous and ignorant Indians are being induced to join this dance which is an injury to them, and you older men who should know better but who have been led into this absurd craze should now stop it and advise the others to return to their homes and make their houses comfortable for winter.

"The annuity clothing will soon be issued and after next ration day if the weather is cold enough I will kill the beef cattle and if everything is as it should be in your camp and the children attending school and the dancing stopped I would wish to have the winter issues of beef put away at J. Carrignan's School, but with the Indians of that settlement continuing the Ghost Dance and only a few children attending the school I could not do so.

"There are many things I would wish to say to you and I am in hopes that you will still listen to me as my advice is for your own good and the good of your people and you should think of your people and of your wives and children. You should advise all Indians to return to their homes and comply with the 'Great Father's' wishes and all will turn out well, but if the Ghost Dance continues much longer there is no knowing what may come from it, as it is in open violation of the department regulations and contrary to the wishes of all friends of the Indians.

"You should remember that the Government was very forgiving and kind to you and your people when destitution and suffering compelled them to come back from the country of the Red Coat (Oglesa) and took them up on the rolls of the different Agencies and have cared for them since as has been done for those who always remained loyal and at peace with the whites, and there is no other Government in the civilized world that would have treated a conquered foe so humanely. Therefore, my friend, listen to this advice and do not attempt to visit any other Agency at present. Do not feel that I dislike you, for I am a firm friend of the Sioux and my greatest desire is that they should be obedient to the will of the 'Great Father' and become a happy and prosperous people.

"I shake hands with you and ask you to accept this advice as it is intended for the good of your people.

"Atayapi Meyelo,

"James McLaughlin,

"*U. S. Indian Agent.*"

FOOTNOTES

[1] See Act of March 2, 1889.

[2] See Appendix No. I.

SITTING BULL AND MAJOR JAMES McLAUGHLIN AT STANDING ROCK

IV

THE MESSIAH DOCTRINE

(TOLD BY MAJOR JAMES MCLAUGHLIN)

The Indian Messiah Doctrine was first heard by the Indians of Standing Rock Agency during the winter of 1888-1889, but was believed in by only a very few of the wilder and non-progressive, and very seldom spoken of after the first few weeks, until about the middle of the past summer, 1890. When reports commenced reaching the agency from the more southern Sioux Agencies, that of Pine Ridge, Rosebud and Cheyenne River, Sioux were organizing (under divine instruction) religious dances preparatory to receiving their dead ancestors and kinsmen, as all dead Indians were returning to re-inhabit the earth, and were then out West in the beautiful mountain valleys (supposed by the Indians to be in Colorado and Wyoming) driving back with them immense herds of buffalo and wild horses; that the Great Spirit was going to annihilate the white race and restore the Indian to his former freedom and happiness, giving back to him his free and independent life.

Sitting Bull, who has always been a disturbing element among the Sioux, has been growing more worthless and insolent the past few months and during the past summer, applied to me several times for permission to visit the southern Sioux Agencies, but the permission being steadily refused, and thus unabled to get away himself, he, on or about October 1, 1890, directed six young men of his followers to proceed to the Minneconjou settlement on the Cheyenne River Reservation, and invite a visit from Kicking Bear, who was reported to have been a year absent from his agency and

35

but recently returned from a visit to the "Ghost Country," having seen all the dead Indians on their way back to rejoin their relatives and also conversed with the new Messiah.

Upon the invitation extended by Sitting Bull, Kicking Bear arrived at this Agency on October 9, 1890, and as Sitting Bull, who had already been apprised of his coming, had everything in readiness for inaugurating the new religious ceremony known among the Indians as the "Ghost Dance," and immediately upon Kicking Bear's arrival, a considerable number of Indians were formally invited and the dance began and continued for several days without cessation.

The following is the substance of the doctrine as expounded by Kicking Bear: Hearing rumors of the dead soon to return to re-inhabit the earth, he, (Kicking Bear) left his home at Cheyenne Agency over a year ago and traveled west as far as he could go by car, where two other Indians (strangers to him but sent on the same mission) joined him, from which point, the three traveled on horse back for four days.

At a point two days out they had passed all signs of white men, no whites having ever reached so far and there they came to a very peculiar looking black man, living alone, who was engaged in making money, spring wagons and buffalo by magic. A few motions of his hand would turn out a large amount of money; a few motions a large amount of spring wagons and ready to hitch to; and a few other passes, a herd of buffalo was sent galloping over the prairie.

On the evening of the fourth day's travel from the end of the railroad, they met a man dressed in Indian costume, with long, golden hair, whose face was beautiful to look upon, and he was first to speak to them, saying, "How, my children. You have done well to make this journey to visit me." He led the way, they following, up a ladder of small clouds and entered the sky through a small round opening and there they were introduced to the Great Spirit and his wife, who were also dressed as Indians. They were shown from this great height all of the countries of the world and saw the old camping grounds, tepees, and dead relatives of all past generations, together with immense herds of buffalo and horses. The

Son of the Great Spirit showed them the wounds in his hands and feet where he had been crucified by the Whites when he first came upon earth, and told them that he was now going to return to the earth but to remain this time with the Indians as his chosen people. Whilst they were talking with the Great Spirit and receiving directions as to how they must instruct their people, a tall, cadaverous looking man with large joints, long teeth and body covered with short hair, entered and said to the Great Spirit, "I want half of the people inhabiting the world." He was answered, "No, I cannot let you have any—I love them all too much." He asked the second time, and was again refused, but, being persistent, he asked a third time, and was then told that the Indians were his chosen people and would not be given up, but that he might have the Whites. The visiting delegation was then informed that the hard looking individual was the person known as the bad spirit (Devil). The Great Spirit then told the visitors that he had neglected the Indians for a long time, but that they would be his special care hereafter, and, and as the earth was getting old and the soil rotten, in many places, with many holes in the surface, he would rebuild the earth by sending a wave of about thirty feet of new soil to cover over the earth, under which all whites would be crushed, but all Indians, believing in the New Religion and practicing the songs and dances, would be suspended in the air as the wave passed over the earth, and that the unbelieving among the Indians would be left in deep ravines and gulches, that would take them several months to find their way out, and that with the wave of new covering, all the Indians who had died would be sent along and re-unite with their kinsmen.

The Great Spirit told them to return to their homes and his Son would accompany them to the end of the railroad and teach them the songs and steps of the new dance on the way; and that they must teach all Indians to practice it constantly, and with true faith, for the longer they doubted and remained unbelievers, the longer would be their delivery and restoration of their dead relatives.

Then they came down the ladder of clouds to where they had left their horses and traveled back, four days journey to the end of the railroad with the "Messiah" hovering over their heads, all the while teaching them the songs and steps to be practiced in the dances. When they reached the railroad, their "Messiah" told them that he would not return to the clouds any more but would remain on the earth and that any Indians dying from that time on would not go to the clouds but go to the ends of the earth and remain there with him until next spring when they would return with all other ghosts to re-inhabit this earth and rejoin their friends. If any person would be killed in endeavoring to carry out this belief, it would be no sacrifice as they would only be a few months separated from their friends in the flesh, until again re-united on this earth.

Kicking Bear first told this fairy tale as if he were one of the three Indians who visited the Great Spirit in the clouds, but afterwards said that he only reached the last settlements among the Utes, where Christ is now residing and preparing his legions of dead Indians to return with him next spring. Here he had met the three Indians who had accompanied the Messiah to the clouds, and conversed with them regarding their trip, and told him all that they had seen as herein related by Kicking Bear.

The absurdity of this doctrine (so pernicious to the average Indian, who, from inherent superstition and desire for their old time freedom are over credulous and ready to believe the most ridiculous absurdities, promulgated by a "Medicine Man"), was easily engrafted upon the Indians notwithstanding the incongruity of what the man of magic was turning out so deftly: Wagons, money and buffalo without stint in quantities to meet the needs and wishes of the Indians. What would they need with money if the other promises were fulfilled? The latter never seemed to enter the minds of the Indians.

The great desire of all Indians to have light wagons and buggies made this feature a catching fake, and buffalo, which is the heart's desire of the Indian, for the excitement of the chase and for the "stomach's sake," capped the climax, and the Indian Millennium was thus hailed with delight, but with great longing and religious preparations.

(*Signed*) J. McLaughlin,

P. S.: I omitted to mention another promise made to the Indians when they visited the Clouds, which was that, when the whites were wiped from the face of the earth on the American continent and only Indians left inhabiting it, the land would be extended further westward by the filling up, for a considerable distance, the ocean on the west, and that it would ever after be made impossible for the whites to navigate the surrounding oceans so as to make a landing on the continent. The Indians would possess the country undisputed and undisturbed for all future time and they would live everlastingly, reinforced by all of their ancestors who had passed to the spirit land during the many past generations. Furthermore, that the secret of making gun powder would be lost to the whites (the recipe taken from them), and that the gun powder now on hand would be worthless when directed against Indians; but that it would kill whites, deer and all kinds of game while the quantity on hand lasted. After which they were to return to bows and arrows as in their days of peace, plenty and happiness.

The foregoing was related to me by "One Bull," nephew of Sitting Bull, (One Bull still lives on the Grand River—1934), and he related it in all seriousness, considering it a greatly sacrilegious act to do so, but he, being a policeman of the Agency at the time, conscientiously considered it his duty to do so.

(*Signed*) J. McLaughlin.

INDIAN POLICEMEN

WHO PARTICIPATED IN THE ARREST OF SITTING BULL AND THE SUBSEQUENT ENGAGEMENT

V

ARREST OF SITTING BULL AUTHORIZED

Since Buffalo Bill had traveled so much with Sitting Bull, the War Department thought this great wild west character could succeed in convincing Sitting Bull to give up the Ghost Dance and disband his followers of the "Messiah Craze." The invitation was extended to Buffalo Bill to attempt this mission, which he promptly accepted. He arrived by train at Bismarck and drove over land to Fort Yates and made ready to visit the camp of Sitting Bull.

To have permitted Buffalo Bill to carry out his plans would have indicated clearly that Major McLaughlin was not able to cope with the situation. Buffalo Bill was on the ground with his retinue of helpers and camp equipment, and in the afternoon of December 13, 1890, started for the Grand River. He went into camp at Oak Creek for the night. The next morning a messenger overtook Buffalo Bill with a dispatch from the War Department, stating that the order to him to bring in Sitting Bull had been canceled. Bill returned to Fort Yates and took no further part in the operations against Sitting Bull.

The new order received from the Department of the Interior directed McLaughlin to work out any plan he thought advisable, and to cooperate with the military authorities at Fort Yates. A plan was worked out with Colonel Drum, commander at the Fort, to send a detachment of soldiers to follow the Indian Police to the camp of the Sioux, and in the event the police could not handle the situation, the military support would come up and surround the camp.

Thirty-eight policemen were ordered to concentrate on the Grand River under the command of Lieutenant Bull Head. On the afternoon of December fourteenth, the military force marched in the direction of the Sioux camp, and camped at night on the bluffs overlooking the Indians about four miles from them. The police surrounded the Sitting Bull cabin just before daylight. When the engagement began, the firing could be plainly heard in the military camp and orders were immediately given for the force to proceed with all possible speed consistent with good order to the scene of the firing. Before the soldiers arrived, however, the engagement was over, and no engagement was in operation except the spasmodic firing of the police at the Indians who escaped up the Grand River.

At the time of this Ghost Dance trouble, Jack Carrignan was a young man and engaged in teaching the Indian school in the Sitting Bull Settlement, and at no time in the proceedings did Carrignan feel it necessary to flee from the scene of the disorder but remained on the job throughout the trouble. He was afterwards Agent of the agency and performed a lifetime of valuable service among the Indians. When he received orders from the Indian Bureau, which he knew were against the best interests of the Indians, he refused to execute the orders and resigned his job. Very few instances of such loyalty to the welfare of the Indians has ever been displayed in the Indian Service.

The orders to make the arrest of Sitting Bull were issued by Major McLaughlin in his own handwriting. The actual order was directed to Lieutenant Bull Head, and enclosed in a letter written by the Major to John Carrignan, the school teacher on Grand River. The letter and the order were copied in the copy book kept by Major McLaughlin. An exact copy of the letter and order of arrest, taken from the copy book, is as follows:

Letter to Carrignan, containing order of arrest and giving details of what steps to take. Letter to Bull Head was enclosed in this letter.

"1:30 P. M.

"Standing Rock,

"December 14, 1890.

"J. M. Carrignan, Esq.,

"Grand River.

"I send a letter by bearer of this to Bull Head ordering him to arrest Sitting Bull tonight. It must be done without fail as the Cavalry will start this evening and will reach the Sitting Bull crossing of Oak Creek tomorrow morning to protect the police from that point into fort. Should by any chance Bull Head be away from Grand River, having started into agency to fix upon a plan of arrest, let Shave Head carry out the order and arrest him as directed in the letter to Bull Head, which you will find herewith. It will hardly be necessary for all the police to come in with Sitting Bull unless they should be opposed by all the infected Indians following them, and after they reach Oak Creek any number can return and keep watch of the other Indians should they attempt to leave the Reservation. Have it announced in the plainest way possible that no other Indians will be disturbed and all will be treated in a kindly manner unless they should attempt to leave the reservation—I trust that the whole police force can be concentrated promptly.

"Very Respectfully,

"James McLaughlin,

"*Indian Agent.*"

"P. S.: Be sure to see that they have a light wagon ready to bring Bull in so that there will be no delay by such an oversight. You had better come in for a time. If Bull Head's wagon is not convenient and they need yours I will see that you are compensated for its use.

"J. McL., *Agent.*"

Letter to Bull Head, enclosed in above letter:

"4:30 P. M.
"Standing Rock,
"December 14, 1890.

"Lieut. Bull Head,
    "Grand River.

    "From reports brought by Sgt. Hawk Man that the time has arrived for the arrest of Sitting Bull and that it can be made by the Indian Police without any risks—I therefore want you to make the arrest before daylight tomorrow morning and try and get back to the Sitting Bull road crossing of Oak Creek by daylight tomorrow morning or as soon after as possible. The Cavalry will leave here tonight and will reach the Sitting Bull crossing on Oak Creek before daylight tomorrow (Monday) morning. Let me hear from you.

    "Louis Primeau will go with the Cavalry as guide and I want you to send a messenger to the Cavalry Command as soon as you can after you arrest him so that they may be able to know how to act in assisting you.

    "Prevent any attempt at a rescue by his party.

    "I have ordered all of the police at Oak Creek to proceed to Carrignan's school to await your orders, this gives you a force of 43 policemen for to use in the arrest.

    "Very respectfully,
        "James McLaughlin,
        "*U. S. Indian Agent.*"

    "P. S.: You must not let him escape."

GRAVE OF SITTING BULL AT FORT YATES, NORTH DAKOTA

VI
THE DEATH OF SITTING BULL

The battle between the Indian Police and the followers of Sitting Bull occurred on the Grand River in South Dakota, about twenty-five miles (airline) Northwest of where the Grand River empties into the Missouri. The conflict took place on the river bottom at the home of Sitting Bull. Beyond the valley, the country is extremely rough and broken by Badlands and washouts. To this day, anyone not familiar with the location would have difficulty locating it. Perhaps a more practical description would be to say that this battlefield is approximately fourteen miles southwest of McLaughlin, South Dakota.

The Grand River was the home of the Hunkpapa Sioux and for generations, most of the noted chiefs, whose names are now familiar to us, were born and raised there, or on the Moreau River to the south. The descendants of this war-like tribe reside at Bull Head, Little Eagle and Thunder Butte, all near the Grand River in South Dakota. In recent years, the Hunkpapas, like other tribes have intermarried, and are located at Fort Yates, Cannon Ball, Selfridge, Shields, Kennel and Fort Totten, all in North Dakota.

The tribe differed in many respects from the other tribes such as the Santees, Minneconjou, and Sans Arc, in appearance, occupation, warfare and even language. The Hunkpapa, in their wild state, were feared by their enemies, for they were fearless fighters, well equipped with battle equipment and horses, and were skilled in waging war. The flanking movements executed by Sherman and Sheridan in the Civil War did not excel the flank

46

attacks of Crazy Horse, administered against Crook and Custer. Necessarily, they possessed a high degree of intelligence, and were great thinkers and philosophers. Since leaving the War Path, they have carried on under our civilization as successfully as many of their White brothers. With all sections of the country asking for Government aid, one wonders whether our civilization has made the Indian more self-supporting. When left alone and unmolested by the White man, the Sioux asked favors from no one. Having trained them assiduously in the ways of the White man, we have taken away that spirit of self-protection that carried them through all adversity.

One of the greatest mistakes ever made by the Government was the Act of Congress opening up ten million acres for settlement on the Standing Rock Reservation. If this great Reservation had been kept intact, with cattle substituted for buffalo, and small gardens and corn for wheat fields, it would not now be necessary for 2,500 Indians on this Reservation, out of a population of 3,700, to ask for Government aid.

Sitting Bull refused to ratify the Act of Congress opening up half of the Standing Rock Reservation to settlement, and did all he could to prevent other Indians from signing. More than three-fourths of the male Indians listened to the commissioners and approved that Act. This action on the part of Indians caused very bad feeling among them, and Sitting Bull felt, no doubt, much humiliated by their approval of the Act. His resistance to the ratification was justified, and time has proven that he was right. For this stand, he deserves the greatest commendation.

He had heard about the Ghost Dance, and tried it as a vehicle in which to ride again to the head of his followers who were deserting him in favor of the Government He was fighting for his country and the leadership of his people. In that struggle he resorted to the weapon he had always used, namely, "Medicine." The "Messiah Craze" afforded him an opportunity to obtain not only new but powerful "Medicine." Through it, he became again the leader of a great number of Indians, many of whom had signed the ratification.

A careful reading of the doctrine of the "Messiah Craze" will reveal how the Story, obtained in the Clouds, wove into one complete code the Story of Christ, the longing of the Indian for peace and happiness, the wrongs of the White man, the relief from hunger and want, and the necessity of following instructions of the teachers. This appealed to every passion of both the wild and the partly civilized Indian. The natural result was to re-establish the position of Sitting Bull, shame those who had opposed him, and finally, induce a great number of Indians to take to the War Path.

There is not any question but what Sitting Bull had the War Path in his mind, and there would no doubt have been a general uprising, had he not been at all times under close observation. It is doubtful whether he believed the Story obtained in the Clouds, but whether or not, he made good use of it to amass his strength against all that was White.

His last moments were filled with tragedy. It was still dark on the morning of December 15, 1890, when the thirty-eight Indian Police, who had been sent by Major McLaughlin to arrest Sitting Bull, surrounded his cabin. Sitting Bull, his two wives, two daughters, one son, and an adopted son, were in the cabin. Sitting Bull was awakened by Lieutenant Bull Head and told to get ready to accompany the police back to Fort Yates. At first, Sitting Bull made no protest, and, apparently, was ready to obey this order. His wives, awakened by the entrance of the police, realized the purpose of the intruders. Undoubtedly, the women were excited, and feared for the life and safety of Sitting Bull and all of his followers. At any rate, they began singing war songs. Crowfoot twitted his father, saying, "When the police or the soldiers are not here, you are brave, but when you see them, you have no courage—you are afraid to fight."

Surrounded by thirty-eight policemen of his own blood, and influenced as he must have been by his wives and his son, he abandoned his intention to surrender. At first, he employed the cunning which was so characteristic of him. He asked for time to have his horse brought from the stable. Here, he gained a few minutes, and in the meantime, his followers, armed with Winchesters, rushed out of their tepees and assembled around Sitting Bull's cabin. By this time, Sitting Bull could restrain his true emotions no longer. Turning on the police, he said, "You are all Indians, and the blood that runs in your veins is the same as mine—you are my own people. I have repeatedly cautioned all Indians to have no faith in the Government. I have refused to give our lands away. Now, they are gone and we have received no pay. My own children now come as agents of that Government to arrest me, and stand ready to shoot down their own flesh and blood to assist that Government. You have no right to do this. You are cowards to come to my house in the night-time. You are dogs to raise your hands against your own people, and you do not deserve to be called Sioux or to live. I call upon my friends to kill you now."

So far as known, these were the last words uttered by the great Medicine Man. Like Cæsar, he turned, and seeing the attacking Brutus, with his dagger raised to be plunged again into his body, could only say, "And you, too, Brutus."

With this command, the shooting began which in a few short minutes left fifteen dead and mortally wounded Sioux on the battle-field. Numbered among them was the body of the great Medicine Man.

SITTING BULL'S TWO WIVES AND TWO DAUGHTERS POSED OUTSIDE THE HOUSE WHERE SITTING BULL
WAS KILLED

Photo by D. F. Barry

VII

AN ACCOUNT OF THE GRAND RIVER TROUBLE

(As told by Major McLaughlin in an
account to the *Northwest Chronicle*.)

"There having been so much said, written and published, during the past few months, of conflicting nature, regarding the late Indian Troubles and present status of the Sioux, and having been one of the earliest subscribers of the *Northwest Chronicle*, in 1866, and acquainted with many of its patrons, I have thought that a brief summary of the facts might be of interest to its readers, hence this article, which is proffered for publication. It may be proper for me to first state that I have been twenty years with the Sioux, in continuous service among them since July 1, 1871; the last ten years of which has been spent at Standing Rock Agency on the 'Great Sioux Reservation;' that I possess knowledge of the Sioux Language to understand and converse fairly well in the vernacular of the tribe; have an extensive acquaintance with the entire Sioux people and a very general knowledge of the Indian Service.

"This by way of preface, now as to the causes of the late disturbance. The causes that led up to the later troubles among the Sioux were numerous, any one of which in itself was insignificant in so far as being sufficient to create any serious disaffection was concerned, but united, by the absurd 'Messiah Craze' proved formidable enough to produce the unsettled state of affairs of the last autumn, which was properly termed an 'Uprising of the Indians.'

"Intending this for a short article I will only go back three years and, therefore, begin with the summer of 1888 when a commission

51

(The Pratt, Wright and Cleveland Commission) visited the Sioux
Agencies, submitted to the Indians for ratification by them, an Act
of Congress which contemplated opening about one-half of the
Sioux Reservation for settlement, and which, under the Sioux
Treaty of 1868 required the signatures of three-fourths of all adult
Indian males interested therein. The Indians were strongly opposed to some of the provisions of the Act and refused to ratify it,
and after three months efforts had failed to obtain the necessary
signatures, negotiations were abandoned and the status of the reservation was unchanged, but a distrustful feeling and fear of some
future legislation that might be detrimental to their interests remained with the Indians. During that fall and before these negotiations referred to had closed, measles broke out among the Indians and was epidemic at all Sioux Agencies throughout the following winter, and an unusual number of deaths resulted.

"The following summer (1889) another commission (the Fos-
ter, Crook and Warren Commission) visited the Sioux and submitted, for their ratification, an Act of Congress approved March 2,
1889, which was more liberal to the Indians in its provisions than
that of the preceding year; and after about three months negotiations the Act was ratified by the commission's having obtained
more than the necessary three-fourths of the signatures of the adult
males interested in the reservation. I regarded this Act liberal in
the main, which, with certain additional provisions conceded by
the Commission before its acceptance by the Indians, and since
ratified by Congressional legislation, I consider just and reasonable and much better for the Sioux than to have retained their large
reservation, and it is thus regarded by the more progressive and
enlightened of the Reservation bands.

"The acceptance of this Act was stubbornly opposed by the non-
progressive class who clung to the old-time ways and Indian life,
and who desired to retain the large reservation intact. Its ratification by the progressive element, opening approximately
10,000,000 acres, engendered bitter feeling between these two factions. Shortly after the ratification of this Act, whooping cough
broke out among the Sioux and legrippe visited them the following

winter, and the great number of deaths resulting cast a gloom over all. The wily Medicine Man (Sitting Bull) proclaimed that it was the manifestation of the displeasure of the 'Great Spirit' at the Indians having accepted the Act, ceding about half of their reservation, which would lead so many of them to abandoning the customs of their ancestors and adopting the ways of the whites.

"Another cause of discouragement was the severe droughts of the past three years throughout the Sioux Reservation, rendering all efforts at agriculture a failure, and many of their stock cattle died of black-leg, added to which was the delay of Congress in making good the promises of the Commission in 1889, together with the fact that whites commenced settling upon the lands they had ceded, which further enabled the non-signers and disaffected element to taunt those who had signed its ratification with having ceded the large tract of land without receiving the compensation promised. These taunts augmented disaffection and counteracted civilizing influences.

"These conditions existed last summer to a greater or less extent at all the Sioux Agencies and the Indians were in a frame of mind when the 'Messiah Doctrine' was announced, it having been brought to the Sioux by three of their tribe who had visited the Shoshones and the Utes, and the malcontents were very ready to accept anything that would unite their different factions in a common cause, and this new doctrine, 'The Indian Millennium,' promised the extinction of the dominant white race and the supremacy of the Indian, had strong fascination for the average uneducated Indian, who is just emerging from barbarism. The new doctrine promised the restoration of the Indian race, the return of buffalo and vast herds of wild horses (to have for the catching), their old life of freedom and excitement of the chase, so dear to their hearts, and their dead relatives were to be reunited with them, as they were all returning to inhabit this continent which would be in the future the country of the Indians, and all this was promised them to take place not later than when the grass was three or four inches high this spring, but in order to bring this about all Indians must be true believers of the new doctrine and practice its admonitions.

This wily and ambitious leader (Sitting Bull), from the steady advancement of the Indians in civilization with individual thinking and acting for themselves independent of their former chiefs, found the power gradually passing from him, and desired it as much at the Agency as on the War Path, saw an opportunity to recover his lost prestige and former popularity by quickly espousing and advocating the new doctrine; and, aided by the shrewd medicine men of the bands who had also been almost lost sight of, immediately posed as prophets, announcing new revelations at regular intervals to enthuse the brethren and keep up interest at the highest. The over-credulous were thus deceived and misled. All Indians who joined the Ghost Dance Craze gave up all interest in everything, other than the dance, abandoned their homes and spent the whole time in practicing its absurdities, except every second Saturday when they reported at the Agencies to receive Government allowances of subsistence and those participating in the dance did so in defiance of orders to the contrary emanating from constituted authority. This was the status of the Ghost Dance Craze and disaffection among the Sioux about the middle of last October (1889).

"I will here say that I do not believe that any evil intentions entered the minds of the larger number of those who participated in the dances when they first joined, (I will not say so much for the leaders, however, who were old time fomenters of disaffection), and if cold weather had set in as early as it usually does in this section, I believe it would have cooled their ardor and frozen out. But the weather continued summer-like and by the middle of December, the dance assumed proportions which called for some action by the authorities, resulting in the death of Sitting Bull on December 15, 1890, and the subjugation of his followers on Pine Ridge Reservation in the affair of Wounded Knee Creek on December 29 (1890)."

VIII

THE MASSACRE ON WOUNDED KNEE CREEK

The agitation concerning the Ghost Dance was not confined to the Standing Rock Reservation. It had spread through the reservations at Crow Creek, Rosebud and Pine Ridge. It spread because there was so much dissatisfaction among the Western Indians, caused by the breaking of treaties, the cutting down of beef issues, in violation of treaty agreements, and things promised by commissioners when the treaties were signed. Besides, the Indians were actually in want and suffering through neglect of the Government, duty bound to protect them as its wards. The Indians, themselves, had never asked to be made wards of the Government. That was wished upon them by the Government, and over which action they as Indians had no voice or control whatever. The Government, then, as now, was under a peculiar duty—a trustee of an express trust—to take care of those who, through no choice of their own, had been made dependents of the Government, and stripped of an equal chance for their own self-protection.

The Wounded Knee engagement occurred just fourteen days after the engagement on Grand River in which Sitting Bull and seven of his followers were killed. The men escaped from the Grand River engagement, and in some instances entire families escaped the police and the soldiers. At the time of the engagement, they were ready to go to Pine Ridge. After this engagement a number of them made their way to Cherry Creek where Big Foot and his band were camped. The distance from the Grand River battleground to

Cherry Creek was approximately ninety miles and the direction nearly south, veering to the west not over fifteen miles.

The camp of Big Foot was already astir with the "Messiah Craze" or "Ghost Dance" dances, and upon the arrival of the refugees from Grand River, full details of the death of Sitting Bull were given. This, naturally, increased the excitement. Big Foot's band were Minneconjou and Sans Arc Sioux. The treatment they had received at the Cheyenne Agency had aroused their resentment against the Government, and Big Foot, upon invitation from Red Cloud, had decided to leave the Cheyenne Agency and go to live at Pine Ridge. The coming of the messengers from the Grand River engagement, increased the desire for Big Foot to be on his way southward. Pine Ridge Agency was some 100 miles south of Cherry Creek and a little over forty miles to the west.

Big Foot employed whatever means he then possessed to make his way to Pine Ridge. On December 22, 1890, Colonel Summer with a troop of cavalry visited the camp of Big Foot and ordered him to move to a camp on the reservation, designated by the Colonel. Big Foot, pretending he was very ill, said that if the soldiers would go ahead and locate the camp, the Indians would follow on the following morning.

If Big Foot obeyed this order, it meant he could not go to join Red Cloud at Pine Ridge. The soldiers left the camp and moved on to prepare a permanent camp for the band. The next day at noon no Indians were in sight and scouts were sent back to contact the Indians. Scouts found the camp deserted and all trace of the trail obliterated.

Instead of following the soldiers, as promised, Big Foot moved out before daylight on the morning of the 23rd in the direction of Pine Ridge. They traveled five days unmolested, but in the meantime troops were scouring the plains and valleys for the whereabouts of this band. On the evening of the 28th, the forces of General James W. Forsyth came in contact with his band on Porcupine Creek.

The events that followed have been told by eyewitnesses, although the records have never been published verbatim. During all the years since this engagement at Wounded Knee, these records of the exact statements taken down at the time have peacefully reposed among the belongings and effects of the late Major McLaughlin, and were turned over to the Author when the publication of this narrative was contemplated.

Philip F. Wells, Interpreter for General James W. Forsyth, in a letter to General Hugh L. Scott, U. S. Army, and James McLaughlin, Inspector, gives a complete account of the events leading up to, during and after the engagement This letter is followed by an article giving the interpreter's own opinion about the matter based upon the facts which were before him. In addition to his statement and opinion, we also include his affidavit and a statement of General James W. Forsyth, respecting the conduct of Phillip Wells during the engagement.

H. L. Scott, General U. S. Army,
Jas. McLaughlin, U. S. Ind. Inspector.
Gentlemen:

In compliance with your request, I am giving you my personal experience and knowledge of different noted events regarding past Indian affairs.

In regard to the Messiah Craze which terminated in the fight at Wounded Knee in 1890-91, I would divide the cause into four different classes. First: In the year 1888 the Indians began to realize that the Black Hills had been taken away from them in violation of treaty laws, which specify that the Government will not take any portion of land away from them without the consent and signature of three-fourths of all male adults over eighteen years old, which would require at the least between 7,000 and 8,000 signatures, whereas the Government secured only 240 some odd signatures. Up to that time the Indians, as yet, had not thought of any hostility, though they were in a disturbed state of mind.

Second: In 1889, General Crook came to them with a Commission and negotiated with them for 11,000,000 acres of land to be ceded to the Government. The Indians were promised by the Commission that if they would sign the treaty, there would not be a cent of reduction made in the provisions and other supplies they were receiving from the Government. But immediately upon the ratification of the treaty by Congress and signature by the President, the beef issue was cut down one-half million pounds and other provisions and supplies at the same ratio.

Third: While the Indians were still angry and excited over having been deceived, a delegation of Indians, from Rosebud and Pine Ridge, who had secretly gone to Walker Lake, Utah, returned with the Message that they had met the Messiah, who had promised them that all the white people would be destroyed, and there would be a resurrection of all the Indians who had died in the past, and their buffalo and all other game would be restored and many other promises, too numerous to mention here. The white settlers, both in South Dakota and Nebraska, upon hearing rumors of this message, misconstrued it to mean that the Indians themselves were going to destroy the white people, instead of the Messiah destroying them as the Indians believed, and began calling for troops to be sent to protect them. The Government responded by sending troops at once and the militia of each state began mobilizing.

Fourth: Referring again to the treaty made by General Crook—it included a clause changing the recognized boundary line between Rosebud and Pine Ridge Indians, which was Pass Creek to Black Pipe, a distance of fifteen miles. A very prominent leading Chief of the Rosebud Indians, by the name of Lip, a number of years before this had moved with his band to the east side of Pass Creek, built up good homes and opened up fields in a very prosperous manner. Because of the change of the boundary line he was left out of the jurisdiction of Rosebud Agency. He objected having to give up his home to move into the Rosebud reservation and demanded that he be transferred to Pine Ridge. In the Crook treaty he was promised that as soon as the treaty was ratified he and his band would be transferred to Pine Ridge, but for some cause or other after ratification of the treaty his transfer was delayed for some time and he became suspicious that he might have to give up his home and move to Rosebud, so as soon as his band heard that the army under command of General Miles, was coming to Pine Ridge, they gathered up all their belongings, including live stock, and moved to Pine Ridge Agency with the express purpose of appealing to General Miles for their transfer. As soon as Lip and his band began to prepare for their move to the Pine Ridge Agency, rumors were spread among the hostile inclined Indians on Rosebud to the effect that Lip and his band were going to move out to the Bad Lands, where it had been secretly agreed a stand would be made and they would fortify themselves for a fight. They all made a quick rush and overtook Lip and his band before they reached the Pine Ridge Agency and by force, tried to take them to the Bad Lands, but Lip succeeded in getting away from them and arrived at the Agency. The hostile Indians continued their course to the Bad Lands, that caused a stampede of the Indians of Pine Ridge, who were similarly inclined and they also rushed to the Bad Lands and began building breastworks and gathering hundreds of head of cattle for their provisions. As yet General Miles had not arrived at the Agency—he came immediately after the fight at Wounded Knee—which left General Brook in command, who was sending out friendly Indians as couriers to the hostile Indians in the Bad Lands, trying to induce them to come to a peace conference, but the Indians sent back replies of stubborn refusal. When Rev. J. J. Jutz, a Catholic priest, in whom the Indians had the utmost confidence, asked permission to be allowed to go to the hostile camps and negotiate peace with them, General Brook granted him the permission and he took with him Jack Red Cloud.

After visiting them and holding conference with them he induced them to surrender under certain conditions and returned to General Brook with a report of these conditions, who approved them. He made a second trip and returned bringing with him all the hostile Indians from the Bad Lands and camped about two or three miles from Pine Ridge Agency. In the meantime, Colonel Summer was ordered out, with a troop of cavalry, to Big Foot's camp on the Cheyenne River to take possession of him and his band to keep them from joining the hostile bands camped in the Bad Lands. Big Foot agreed to surrender and move with his band to a camp designated by the Colonel, but asked permission to wait until the following morning because he was ill. He told Colonel Summer that if he would go ahead and decide on and prepare a place he, Big Foot, and his band would come on the next morning, to which Colonel Summer agreed and moved on to locate camp. The next day Colonel Summer waited until about noon and then ordered scouts out to meet Big Foot and his band to guide them to camp. The scouts could find nothing of them and proceeded until they reached the camp where they found them gone with no trace left.

Report was immediately sent to General Brook at Pine Ridge that Big Foot had escaped from Colonel Summer and was presumably heading for the hostile Indians in the Bad Lands. Major Whiteside with a portion of the Seventh cavalry was ordered out to intercept him and disarm him before he could reach the hostile Indians. In the evening of December 28, 1890, Major Whiteside sent in a report to General Brook that he had captured Big Foot and his band and had gone into camp at Wounded Knee, and that night the balance of the Seventh cavalry with a full detachment of Captain Taylor's scouts were sent out to Wounded Knee.

* * *

North Dakota

South Dakota

ADAMS

HETTINGER

PERKINS

CAMPBELL

WALWORTH

EMMONS

LINTON

DEWEY

ARMSTRONG

POTTER

SULLY

HUGHES

STANLEY

WASHABAUGH

MELLETTE

BENNETT

WASHINGTON

Pierre

Fort Pierre

Milwaukee

As to further description of the fight I herewith, enclose a statement of General Forsyth and also statements
of some Indians wounded in the fight (statements taken
at the hospital), and my statement and also two newspaper clippings—one of them written and published shortly
after the fight, which was a very misleading statement,
and again published in 1913 after the moving pictures were
taken at Pine Ridge and the other my reply to the same
which shows the position of the troops.

Respectfully,

Philip F. Wells.

Kadoka, South Dakota,

September 3, 1920.

MY PERSONAL OPINION BASED ON FACTS:

In addition to the causes I have already stated, the
Indians, being in such a hostile state of mind, and the
ghost dance taking possession of them, became fanatics.

While things were at this state, a change in administration at Washington occurred—a grave mistake on the
part of the Indian office to change the agent and other
employees for entirely inexperienced men, when on Pine
Ridge things were at such a crisis. Whilst in my opinion,
the agent and other employees were honest, well-mean-
ing men, their incompetency caused them to lose control
of the Indians, while experienced men may have been able
to handle the situation. I will mention the work of two
experienced men, Rev. Amos Ross, Episcopal Missionary
(an Indian mixed blood), and myself. I was farmer in
charge of the Medicine Root district, the only district
farmer left of the old employees. Rev. Ross and I outlined
our work in this way. He called all his church followers
and other intelligent Indians that he could control and
conferred with them and I conferred with my policemen and the leading Indians I could control. In that way

we united the government work and church work and exercised a good influence over the Indi-ans and kept the ghost dance entirely out of my district—the only district on Pine Ridge reservation free from the ghost dance and kept under perfect discipline.

Rev. Moss and I both agreed with the Indians that we would not resort to any force if the ghost dance were to start in my district, that we and our followers would go in person to all their gatherings and insure them we would not interfere in their religious liberty as long as they did not interfere with school or violate other laws. The inexperienced agent at Pine Ridge was like a drowning man who clutches at a straw, and was ready to take the first advice given him which was not always the wisest, and moved me from the district to the agency where he was advised my services were more needed, and, thereby, left me helpless in my work of controlling the Indians.

Commenting on Col. Summer's action, allowing Big Foot's escape on the Cheyenne, he was subjected to severe criticism from both army and civilians. However, there were good reasons for his leniency. In my opinion he thought it the better way to put them on their honor and thereby control them peaceably, in that way acting in accordance with explicit orders from the President, and carried out by General Miles in all his orders, to use every possible means to avoid bloodshed when handling the Indians.

Commenting on Colonel Forsyth in the fight at Wounded Knee, he was as severely and unjustly criticized for the drastic measures he used in dealing with the Indians as Colonel Sumner was for his leniency. Having in view the treacherous way in which Big Foot had deceived Colonel Sumner, Colonel Forsyth would take no chances with them but strongly insisted on Big Foot being disarmed in obedience to his orders. Colonel Forsyth was blamed for so many women and children being killed which was deplorable enough and equally unjust.

As the ghost shirts worn by both men and women were the same it was impossible to distinguish between them and the men were shooting at the soldiers from among the women. Most of the soldiers had never seen an Indian before and the smoke from the black powder used, was so dense and the dress so similar it would have been difficult for one familiar with the Indians to make a distinction. At the time, many misleading statements were made—like those in the accompanying newspaper clipping, and others about the officers and soldiers being drunk and mistreating the Indians and exasperating them into fighting, which were all absolutely false. Even the author of the history of South Dakota has been misled into making similar statements. The first fire the women and children were exposed to, was from the Indians themselves as Wallace's troops was drawn up between the body of Indians and the camp where the women and children were and in order to gain the canyon the Indians fired upon Wallace's troop directly in front of their camp. Most of the soldiers killed were of Wallace's troop and he with them. I can positively say I saw no act of unkindness by either the officers or men toward the Indians and the enclosed statements of wounded Indians show they were treated only with kindness. My different acts of kindness towards the wounded Indians, as stated by them, were all at the orders of Colonel Forsyth.

I noticed in your work you have taken statements of William Garnett and Baptiste Pourier, of Pine Ridge Indian reservation, South Dakota, and wish to state I have been personally and intimately acquainted with them for about thirty-five years and know them to be excellent interpreters of the Sioux language, well informed as to matters that have transferred among the Oglala Sioux for many years past and the truthfulness of their statements regarding said Indians for the past fifty years cannot be questioned.

Respectfully,

Philip F. Wells.

Kadoka, South, Dakota,

Sept. 3, 1920.

This was not submitted with my report of January 12, 1921, Mr. Wells' letter of September 3, 1920, being regarded ample to such requirements.

A half-bred, P. F. Wells being duly sworn, testified as follows:

I was Interpreter for Colonel Forsyth—at the time of battle on Wounded Knee, December 29th, 1890. Colonel Forsyth spoke to Big Foot through me as follows:—you tell Big Foot that he tells me that his Indians had no arms, when yesterday at time of surrender they were all well armed, I am sure that he is deceiving me, tell him, Big Foot that he need have no fear in giving up his arms as I wish to treat you with nothing but kindness.

Have I not done enough for you to convince you that I intend nothing but kindness. Did I not put you into an ambulance and treat you kindly, and put you into a good tent, and put a stove into it to keep you warm and comfortable, and I have sent off to get provisions for your people which I expect here before long so that I can feed you well, and I have had my Doctors taking care of you.

Then Big Foot answered, they have no guns, only such as you have found, ("which I, the Interpreter, saw was about a dozen old rifles, tied up with strings, different old fashioned rifles, not a decent one in the lot.") I gathered up all my guns at the Cheyenne River Agency and turned them in and they were all burned up. Then

General Forsyth answered you are lying to me in return for all my kindness to you Big Foot answered in substance as before: At this time the soldiers were searching again.

During this time a medicine man, all painted up and fantastically dressed, was going on with a silent ghost dance or rather the maneuvers of the ghost dance worship, throwing up his hands and occasionally picking up dust and throwing it towards the soldiers, who are standing in ranks around; then he turned toward the young bucks, who were squatted together, and said do not be afraid and let your hearts be strong, to meet what is before you—we are all well aware that there are lots of soldiers about us and they have lots of bullets, but I have received assurance that their bullets can not penetrate us. The prairie is large and the bullets will not go towards you but over the large prairies, and if they do go towards you, they will not penetrate you.

Then all these young bucks answered "how" with great earnestness, this meaning that they were with him, or would stand by him, I then turned to Major Whitside and said that man is making mischief, and repeated to him what he had said. He said go direct to General Forsyth and tell him about it, which I did. So he came along with me to the edge of the Indian circle of bucks and told me to tell that man to sit down and keep quiet, the man then being engaged again in silent maneuvers or incantations. But he kept on and paid no attention to the order. When General Forsyth repeated the order—and when I translated it in Indian, Big Foot's brother-in-law said—he will sit down when he gets around the circle—and when he reached the end, he squatted down. At the end of General Forsyth's conversation through me to Big Foot, the brother-in-law asked that they be allowed to take their chief, Big Foot, "who is dying" and go amongst our people, meaning to continue on the journey they had been making before the arrest: The General answered, I can take better care of him than you can any where, as I have my Doctor tending to him—Then General Forsyth went to one side giving instructions elsewhere, this was after I had told him that the medicine man was inciting trouble—after the medicine man sat down, some Sergeant of Cavalry said to General Forsyth, their goes one with a gun under his blanket—the Indian was walking around the circle.

The General ordered the Sergeant to take it away from the Indian and he went up and snatched the rifle away from him. Then Major Whitside said to me tell the Indians that it is necessary that they should be searched one at a time. This while he stood to one side with five or six soldiers. The Indians or rather the old ones assembled willingly by answering "how" and the search began whilst the young bucks paid no attention at all, the old ones, that were sitting next to us, passed through, (some five or six of them) and submitted to the search—whilst this was going on I kept a watch on the medicine man for fear of a row and then I heard some one to my left call out "look out, look out," and that instant, as I turned my head I brought my arms to a "port" and then saw five or six young bucks throw off their blankets and pull out their arms from under them, brandish them in the air, and immediately the older Indians that were sitting between us and the younger ones, rose up so that the farther end of circle, some forty feet away, was hidden from my view. I heard a shot fired from the midst of them and as I started to cock my rifle throwing my eyes to the right to see the treacherous fellow when I suspected, he had, or some one like him from that lot, come to within 3 or 4 feet of me; with a long cheese knife, ground to a sharp point, raised to stab me. Then the fight between him and me prevented me from seeing anything else at the time, he stabbing me by cutting off the end of my nose, and I keeping him off till I

could swing my rifle to hit him, which I finally succeeded
in doing, and I then shot and killed him as soon as I had
room to aim my rifle. By this time the fight between the
Indians and soldiers had become general.

Up to that time the women and children in and around
the tepees were not fired at until some five or six of the
bucks ran amongst the women and children and began
firing from there, and the fire of the soldiers was directed
towards them. This was all that I saw positively, as I was
bleeding profusely and was led off, my senses having almost left me—after the heavy fight was over, I came back
to where the dead and wounded were lying motionless and
called out these white people came to save you and you
have brought death on yourselves. Still white people are
merciful to save the wounded enemy when he is harmless, so if some of you are alive, raise your heads—I am a
man of your own blood who is talking to you." At this
about a dozen-heads were raised from among those that
were seemingly dead—one man especially raised himself
on his elbow and said "are you the man they call Fox" (my
Indian name.) I told him I was—He says I want you to
favor me by coming to me. I suspected him however and
raising my gun went towards him. He says who is that
man lying burned there, meaning an Indian who had run
into a scouts tent; and who had from there killed three or
four soldiers, until they—the soldiers had fired a volley
into the same and had finally set the tent on fire to get
him out.

I supposed he was one of the two medicine men and
replied accordingly. He raised himself a little higher,
raised his closed fist pointing it towards the dead Indian,
shot out his fingers, which is amongst Indians a deadly
insult meaning—I could kill you and be satisfied doing it,
am sorry I could do no more to you, and then used words
trembling, but which I could not all catch, but he said this
which I did hear, speaking as though—to the dead man

"if I could be taken to you I would stab you," then turning to me said "he is our murderer, only for him inciting our other young men we would have been all alive and happy." And an old woman, whom I was conducting to a safe place, told me "the treacherous ones are of Big Foot's band, these two medicine men have been trying constantly to incite the others to trouble since we, of Humps band, have been with them—some of us honestly want peace when we raised the white flag. But in spite of that, trouble has been made—some of the women that were wounded said about the same thing. Before this while some of the soldiers were still firing, I heard General Forsyth yelling "quit shooting at them," this in efforts to save women and children and the firing towards them ceased, some soldier replied, that fellow—alluding to a wounded buck among the women—is raising a gun to shoot—an instant or two before I heard a similar order given, but I heard General Forsyth's order distinctly, and the soldiers reply as though in excuse for his action in disobedience of the first orders.

(A True Copy)

J. Ford Kent,

Lt. Col. 18th Inf., A. I. G.

HEADQUARTERS 7 CAVALRY

Ft. Riley, Kansas, March 5, 1891.

The Adjutant General, U. S. A.,

Washington, D. C.

(Through Headquarters, Department of the Missouri).

Sir:

I have the honor to invite especial attention to the conduct of Interpreter, Philip Wells, at the battle of Wounded Knee, South Dakota, December 29th, 1890, and the engagement near Drexel Mission, South Dakota, December 30, 1890.

Mr. Wells accompanied Lieutenant Taylor's Troop
of Scouts, to which he was attached as Interpreter, to
Wounded Knee with my command on the evening of
December 28th, 1890. During the council the next morning he rendered every assistance in his power to overcome
the disinclination of the Indians to turn in their arms. He
was within the circle of the Indians when the outbreak
took place and was at once stunned by a blow from an
Indian from behind. He quickly recovered himself, and
turning, saw the Indian in the act of striking him with a
large knife. This blow he partially avoided by raising his
arm, as it struck him in the face and nearly severed his
nose, leaving only a small portion of flesh by which it was
held to his face. Clubbing the Indian with the barrel of
his gun to gain the necessary time to step back, he took
deliberate aim and killed the buck. Hastening to the Surgeon he waited only long enough to have his face partly
covered with cotton to stop the flow of blood, and then
return with his gun, took an active part in the remainder
of the fight, in fact, he could have rendered no better service if he had not received the wound.

He rode with the column on his return that night to
the Agency, ready for any duty. Early the next morning,
while waiting in the Division Hospital to have his wound
attended to, the alarm regarding the Drexel Mission was
received and the Seventh Cavalry ordered out, Mr. Wells
without waiting for surgical attention, ran out of the hospital and jumped on the first pony he could find and accompanied the Regiment during the entire day.

I consider Interpreter Wells' conduct during the two
days as remarkably fine and gallant and urgently recommend him for the substantial reward that can be given
him.

Very respectfully,
(*Signed*) James W. Forsyth,
Colonel Seventh Cavalry.

HEADQUARTERS 7 CAVALRY

I now present the signed statements of three of the warriors who were with Big Foot's Band and went through the entire engagement. These statements come from "Help Them," an Ogalala Sioux, from "Catching Spirit Elk," and from "Frog," a brother of Big Foot.

"Help Them"

Pine Ridge Agency, S. D.,

January 7th, 1891.

Statement of "Help Them."—Son of "Heart Man," living on Wounded Knee, Pine Ridge reservation.

—o—

I am an Ogalala, I went on a visit to "Big Foots" camp on Cheyenne River, and as I was on my way home, I came along with "Big Foots" people. When we were taken by the soldiers (day before the fight at Wounded Knee) we were treated kindly by them: We were given provisions to eat.

The only thing that did not look friendly on the part of the soldiers was, they kept their guns in readiness for action, and when we came into camp they placed two canons on a hill covering our camp, the men were not allowed to take the horses to water, so the watering of the horses was done by little boys.

To the best of my knowledge the Indians had no intention of fighting. The disarming of the Indians had begun peaceably by some of them, I had given up my gun, and left the circle, and was going towards our camp where all the women and children were.

For some time before that, the "Medicine" man had been going around, going through the maneuvers of the "ghost dance." He stopped, turned around facing a crowd of young Indians, (who were standing together, with their guns concealed under their blankets), and spoke to them, but I could not hear what he said, though I heard them all answer "How."

Shortly after I heard a white man saying something in excited tones, which I could not understand and looking around I saw some of the Indians, throw off their blankets, and raise their guns one of the Indians fired a shot, I did not recognize him, as I turned around, I heard a few shots following the first, then the firing began so fast, I could not tell what happened after that.

The "Medicine" man, had been telling the Indians all the way, that the soldiers bullets could not reach them (The Indians), no matter how the soldiers would shoot at them.

(*Signed*) Charles Smith Cook,
Missionary of the Episcopal Church.
(*Signed*) P. F. Wells.
   (A true copy)
   J. Ford Kent,
   Lt. Col. 18th Inf., A. I. G.

Statement of Catching Spirit Elk
(Hehakawanyakapi)

Age 38, of Hump's band. A ghost dancer. I came along with Big Foots' Band as by an accident, namely; We heard that Big Foots and people were invited to come and live here with the Ogalalas. I joined them, being myself an Ogalala. Fifth day out we met the soldiers. We were just coming down the hills beyond Porcupine Tail Creek, when we were met by four scouts. I saw only one, *Highbackbone*, the others riding back rapidly to tell the soldiers of our coming. I asked the scout the object of his coming to us. He answered, "we heard you were coming and so have come to meet you. Everything will be all right." We got into Porcupine Tail Creek and made coffee there. Then we came on, preceded by our horsemen. Presently it was said, "Soldiers are coming?" I looked and saw them coming, making much dust. They came on and finally halted at a given place not far from us. We still came on toward them, preceded by our horsemen. On a little rise they placed two cannon covering us, having their other guns in readiness for firing. We came right on towards them and finally reached them, our people saying, "They are only fooling us." We finally mingled together with them, and came on with them, some of the soldiers preceding us and the rest coming on behind. We reached the Wounded Knee, we camped right by their side. Of course we were guarded. It was a lonely coming. Rations were soon given us and everything seemed friendly. There being no bad intentions on our part, we didn't entertain any sense of fear. There was no suspicion on our part towards the soldiers. We were simply coming this way because of the invitation from Red Cloud, Young-man, Afraid of His Horse, and other chiefs.

We did not ask for the usual *passes* because we knew we would be refused. At the Wounded Knee the men *were* not allowed to take the horses to water. The boys had charge of that. Even then I did not think that we were under suspicion. After breakfast, that morning, I went out and learned that all the men were wanted at a given place. I went to it near Big Foot's tent, which was near the soldiers. It was then said that all our guns were wanted. Many of the soldiers, (cavalry) were arranging themselves into positions; and the infantry came on between us and the women and children. All the *men* were thus separated from the women. I heard an officer saying something. He must have given orders, because the soldiers began loading their guns and holding them in readiness for firing. I called out and said, "Let us give up every gun." I said this because I thought it was best to do so. Many were brought. Can not say exactly how many, but thought all had been gathered up. Every man in the Indian party did not have a gun. I gave up my Winchester, which was all that I had.

A man by name Hose-Yanka (a rascally fellow) was at this juncture "making medicine," but I did not hear what he was saying. Also about this time a more rigid searching of the Indians was instituted. When they came to me I gave up my cartridge belt. A soldier took it and began taking off the cartridges, apparently to return to me the belt, so I stood by him waiting for it. Just then I heard the report of a gun and saw a man throwing off his sheet-covering then followed firing from all sides. I threw myself on the ground. I then jumped up to run towards the Indian camp, but was then and there shot down, being hit on my right leg and soon after was shot again on the other leg.

When the general firing ceased I heard an interpreter, calling out, saying the wounded would be kindly treated. I opened my eyes and looked about and saw the dead and wounded all around me. Five men and Mrs. Big Foot were near me, alive. My wife and younger child, I hear were not killed; but my older girl is missing. Alec Adams, Government herder here, is my brother.

The young man who fired the first gun is the one who brought all this trouble upon us.

(*Signed*) Chas. Smith Cook

P. F. Wells

Copied from Mr. Cook's paper by his wife.

Pine Ridge Agency, S. D.

January 7th, 1891

Statement of Frog (of Big Foot's Band)

I am a brother of "Big Foots." We, "Big Foots band," left Cheyenne river where we had been living. As "Big Foot" was tired of the bad treatment he had been getting, at the hands of both Indians and white people, and besides we (Big Foots band) had been asked at different times during the summer, by "Red Cloud," "Little Wound,"

"Afraid of His Horses," and "No Water," to come to Pine Ridge Agency and join them.

From the time we left home, till we came to Pine Ridge reservation, we had not been interfered with by soldiers, or any one else. When we were taken by the soldiers, (the day before the fight at Wounded Knee), they treated us with nothing but kindness and brought us to camp.

The following morning, the soldiers began blowing their bugles, and began to stand around us, in ranks, but I thought nothing of it, as it was their natural customs to do so, and then we were told (all of us men) to come out and sit down, at a place near the door of "Big Foots" tent, which we did.

Then a lot of soldiers got in between us (the men), and our camp, separating us, (the men) from the women and children. An officer then told us he wanted our guns, and as soon as we gave them up, we had all given them up as I thought, when I saw an Indian with a gun under his blanket, and the soldiers saw it at the same time, and they took it away from him, they (the soldiers) commenced searching the Indians at the same time, meanwhile the Medicine man, was going through the incantations of the ghost dance, stopped and began speaking to the younger Indians, but I paid no attention to what he said, as I had not the least fear of any trouble, so I pulled my blanket over my head, and did not see anything, until I heard much talking and loud voices, I uncovered my head, and I saw every one had arisen on his feet and I heard a shot coming, from where the young Indians stood, shortly after that I was shot down, I laid there as I fell, the firing was so fast, and the smoke and dust so thick, I did not see much more of the fight until it was over. I heard some one saying, "Indians, all of you who are yet alive, raise your heads, the white men do not wish to kill you." I raised my head and saw a man standing among the dead, and I asked him if he was the man they called "Fox" and he said he was and I said, "will you come to me?" and he came to my side.

I then asked him who is that man lying there half burned, and he said I understand it is the Medicine man, and I threw at him (the Medicine man) my most bitter hatred and contempt. I then said to "Fox," he has caused the death of all our people.

(*Signed*) Charles Smith Cook,

Missionary of the Episcopal Church.

(*Signed*) P. F. Wells.

(A true copy).

J. Ford Kent,

Lt. Col. 18th Inf., A. I. G.

APPENDIX NO. 1

The following letter relating to the release of Sitting Bull from Fort Randall was written by Major McLaughlin to the Commissioner of Indian Affairs.

Fort Yates, Dakota, February 15, 1883.
Hon. H. Price, Commissioner of Indian Affairs.
Dear Sir:

I have the honor to state that Sitting Bull, who is now held by the military at Ft. Randall, D. T., as a prisoner of war, has applied to me several times, during the past year, for intercession in his behalf, and that he, and his people, who are prisoners with him, be transferred to the Interior Department and be located on the Grand River at the Standing Rock Agency in Dakota.

I am now informed that the military authorities have no objection to such transfer as the Indians of Standing Rock Agency are closely related to the Sitting Bull prisoners. They are very willing to aid them by sharing their supplies and assist in planting next spring. I would, therefore, respectfully suggest (if it is the intention of the Interior Department to place them at the Standing Rock Agency) the propriety of sending them up the Missouri River by one of the first steamboats in the spring, which would be about the middle of April next, and which would enable them to plant some crops the coming season, this

77

placing them as not entirely dependent upon subsistence issues by the Government. Should their arrival at the Agency be delayed later than the first week in May, there would be a whole year lost to them before they could do anything towards helping themselves.

In view of the facts and having the utmost confidence in the good intentions of Sitting Bull, I would respectfully recommend early action in bringing about the transfer of these people.

Very respectfully,

James McLaughlin.

The following correspondence relating to the granting of permission to Sitting Bull and a few of his followers to travel with Buffalo Bill and his Wild West Show was received by Major McLaughlin from officials in Washington:

WAR DEPARTMENT

Washington, D. C., May 18, 1885.

To Agent McLaughlin,

Ft. Yates, North Dakota.

Secretary authorizes Sitting Bull and a few of his Indian friends to travel through the East in charge of F. W. Cody.

E. L. Stevens,

Acting Commissioner.

DEPARTMENT OF THE INTERIOR

Washington, D. C., May 18.

The Commissioner of Indian Affairs.

Sir:

In accordance with the recommendations contained in your communication of this date, authority is hereby granted for Sitting Bull and a few of his Indian friends to travel through the East with F. W. Cody (Buffalo Bill) in accordance with the papers herewith returned favorably endorsed by General W. T. Sherman, retired, and Colonel Carr of the Army.

Very respectfully,
L. Q. C. Lamar,
Secretary.

OFFICE OF COMMISSIONER OF INDIAN AFFAIRS
Washington, D. C., May 18, 1885.

To Agent McLaughlin,
Ft. Yates, Dakota:

Secretary authorizes Sitting Bull and a few of his Indian friends to travel through the East in charge of W. F. Cody.

Charge Indian Office,
E. L. Stevens,
Acting Commissioner.

APPENDIX NO. 2

There follows in this Appendix the file of official correspondence of Major McLaughlin regarding the death of Sitting Bull.

Fort Yates, June 18, 1890.

Gen'l. Ruger,
    St. Paul, Minn.
    These Indians quiet and manifest no interest in Northern Cheyenne troubles. Police are vigilant and will arrest any envoy arriving.
    McLaughlin,
    Agent.
O. B. and Paid Govt. Rate.
(Copy Telegram)

Standing Rock Agency, June 18, 1890.

Hon. T. J. Morgan, Commissioner of Indian Affairs,
    Washington, D. C.
Sir:
    I have the honor to acknowledge the receipt of Office Letter "L", dated the 7th instant, which inclosed copy of a letter from Charles L. Hyde, of Pierre, South Dakota, giving the information which he states has come to him through a source that he has confidence in, that the Sioux Indians or a portion of them are secretly planning and

arranging for an outbreak in the near future. In reply I desire to state that in so far as the Indians of this Agency are concerned there is nothing in either their words or actions that would justify the rumor and I do not believe that such an imprudent step is seriously meditated by any of the Sioux. I have been 19 days of the past five weeks engaged in visiting the Indians of this Agency at their respective homes remaining overnight in Indian houses, in distant settlements, wherever night overtook me, and I found a warm welcome everywhere and the best possible state of feeling prevailing among them.

I possess sufficient knowledge of the Sioux language to understand and converse fairly well in the vernacular of the tribe, and no sign, word or act was noticed during my recent tour among these Indians that would lead me to suspect any dis-contentment among them. There are, however, a few mal-contents here, as at all of the Sioux Agencies, who cling tenaciously to the old Indian ways and are slow to accept the better order of things, whose influence is exerted in the wrong direction, and this class of Indians is ever ready to circulate idle rumors and sow dissentions to discourage the more progressive, but only a very few of the Sioux could now possibly be united in attempting any overt act against the Government, and the removal from among them of a few individuals (the leaders of disaffection) such as Sitting Bull, Circling Bear, Black Bird and Circling Hawk, of this Agency; Spotted Elk and his lieutenants of Cheyenne River; Crow Dog and Low Dog of Rosebud, and any of like ilk of Pine Ridge, would end all trouble or uneasiness in the future.

By far the larger number of the Sioux are well disposed, and there are at this Agency some very reliable and trustworthy Indians, whose sincerity and truthfulness is of a high order and in my investigating what grounds, if any, there were for the rumor of a contemplated outbreak, I talked with several confidentially in regard to the matter and each replied that any fears of an uprising were entirely groundless, and assured me that if such was being meditated by even a few, it could not be kept a secret from them.

There are also, on our Police Force, some excellent men upon whom I can implicitly rely, and I have instructed them to be doubly vigilant and report to me everything learned at home or from other Agencies, and should anything of importance come to my knowledge I will advise you promptly.

I have, however, every confidence in the good intentions of the Sioux as a people.

They will not be the aggressors in any overt act against white settlers, and if *justice* is only done them no uneasiness need be entertained.

I am, Sir,

Very respectfully,

Your obedient servant,

James McLaughlin,

U. S. Ind. Agt.

Standing Rock Agency,
October 17, 1890.

Hon. T. J. Morgan,

Commissioner of Indian Affairs, Washington, D. C.

Sir:

Referring to the subject of Office letter "L," dated June 7th last and my reply of the 18th of same month relative to rumors of a prospective outbreak among the Sioux, I have the honor to state that there is now considerable excitement and some disaffection existing among certain Indians of this Agency at the present time.

I trust that I may not be considered an alarmist and believe that my past record among the Sioux will remove any doubt in this respect and I do not wish to be understood as considering the present state of excitement so alarming as to apprehend any immediate uprising or serious outcome, but I do feel it my duty to report the present "craze" and nature of the excitement existing among the "Sitting Bull" faction of Indians over the expected "Indian Millenium," the annihilation of the white man, and supremacy of the Indian, which is looked for in the near future and promised by the Indian "Medicine Men" as not later than next spring, when the new grass begins to appear, and is known among the Sioux as the "return of the Ghosts."

They are promised by some members of the Sioux tribe, who have lately developed into "Medicine Men," that the Great Spirit has promised them that their punishment by the dominant race has been sufficient and that their numbers having now become so decimated will be rein-forced by all Indians who are dead; that the dead are all returning to re-inhabit this earth which belongs to the Indians; that they are driving back with them as they re-turn, immense herds of buffalo and elegant wild horses to have for the catching; that the Great Spirit promises them that the white man will be unable to make gunpow-der in future and all attempts at such will be a failure and that the gunpowder now on hand will be useless as against Indians, as it will not throw a bullet with sufficient force to pass through the skin of an Indian; that the Great Spirit has deserted the Indians for a long period but is now with them and against the whites, and will cover the earth over with thirty feet of additional soil, well sodded and tim-bered, under which the whites will all be smothered, and any whites who may escape this great phenomena will become small fishes in the rivers of the country, but in order to bring about this happy result the Indians must do their part and become believers and thoroughly organized.

It would seem impossible that any person, no matter how ignorant, could be brought to believe such absurd

nonsense, but as a matter of fact a great many Indians of
this Agency actually believe it, and since this new doctrine has been engrafted here from the more southern
Sioux Agencies the infection has been wonderful, and so
pernicious that it now includes some of the Indians who
were formerly numbered with the progressive and more
intelligent and many of our very best Indians appear
"dazed" and undecided when talking of it, their inherent
superstition having been thoroughly aroused.

"Sitting Bull" is high priest and leading apostle of this
latest Indian absurdity; in a word he is the Chief Mischief
Maker at this Agency, and if he were not here this craze
so general among the Sioux would never have gotten a
foothold at this Agency. "Sitting Bull" is a man of low cunning, devoid of a single manly principle in his nature or
an honorable trait of character, but on the contrary is
capable of instigating and inciting others (those who believe in his powers) to do any amount of mischief. He is a
coward and lacks moral courage, he will never lead where
there is danger but is an adept in influencing his ignorant henchmen and followers, and there is no knowing
what he may direct them to attempt.

He ("Sitting Bull") is bitterly opposed to having any
surveys made on the reservation and is continually agi-
tating and fostering opposition to surveys among his followers, who are the more worthless, ignorant, obstinate
and non-progressive of the Sioux.

He has announced that those who signed the Agreement ratifying the Act of March 2nd, 1889, opening the
Sioux reservation will be compelled to accept a smaller
corner to be set apart and subdivided into small tracts
for them to settle upon, where they will be obliged to remain and support themselves, but those who have refused
to ratify the Act, or, who have ratified, will now oppose
surveys and refuse to accept allotments, will have all the
unoccupied portion of the reservation to hold in common
and continue to enjoy their old Indian ways and former

freedom and therefore will have to be rationed by the Government for all time to come, and it is not to be greatly wondered at that, among an uneducated and ignorant people, he finds supporters and admirers.

He is an Indian unworthy of notice except as a disaffected intriguer, who grasps every opportunity to maintain his power and popularity. He is opposed to everything of an elevating nature and is the most vain, pompous and untruthful Indian that I ever knew. His word is not believed by the more intelligent Indians of this Agency but he has unfortunately, a tribal reputation gained by the generalship of others and is therefore the idol of the disaffected and worthless element of the Sioux. He has been growing bolder and more aggressive throughout the past year and it is undoubtedly only a question of time (a few months at the most) until it will be necessary to remove him from among his people, and I believe that if we can even tide over the present craze without removing him from the reservation it will be necessary to deal with him in a summary manner as soon as the survey of this reservation commences. He is such an abject coward that he will not commit any overt act or open offense himself, but does the intriguing and directs the mischief to be done by his less cunning followers.

In this connection I would respectfully invite attention to my letter of June 18th last, wherein I referred to the character of Sitting Bull and certain others of his supporters and suggested that should their future conduct justify it they be removed from among the Sioux, giving the names of Sitting Bull, Circling Bear, Black Bird and Circling Hawk, of this Agency, as fit subjects for such discipline and I am forced to the belief that to insure peace and to promote the welfare of the Sioux people, such removal will sooner or later be found necessary.

Sitting Bull is a polygamist, libertine, habitual liar, active obstructionist and a great obstacle in the civilization of these people and he is so totally devoid of any of

the nobler traits of character and so wedded to the old
Indian ways and superstitions that it is very doubtful if
any change for the better will ever come over him at his
present age of 56 years. He has been a disturbing element
here since his return from confinement as a military prisoner, in the spring of 1883, but has been growing gradually worse for the past year, which is partly to be ac-
counted for by the presence of a lady from Brooklyn,
N. Y., named Mrs. C. Weldon, who came here in June,
1889, announcing herself as a member of Dr. Bland's
Society, the Indian Defense Association, and opposed to
the Indians ratifying the Act of March 2, 1889, demanding of me permission to pass through the Sioux reservation to Cheyenne River Agency and to take Sitting Bull
with her. The Sioux Commission being then engaged ne-
gotiating with the Indians at the Southern Sioux Agencies, I, as a matter of course refused to permit her either
to pass through the reservation or allow Sitting Bull to
accompany her and compelled her to cross the Missouri
River at this point and travel over the public roads outside of the reservation, in consequence of which she was
very hostile towards me and wrote several letters to different parties in condemnation of my course and action.
While here she bestowed numerous presents upon Sitting
Bull, considerable being money, which had a demoralizing effect upon him, inflating him with his importance.

After her departure she kept up a correspondence with
Sitting Bull until early last spring when she again returned
and located on the north bank of Cannon Ball River just
outside of this reservation and about 25 miles north of
the Agency. Sitting Bull has been a frequent visitor to her
house and he has grown more insolent and worthless with
every visit he has made there; her lavish expenditure of
money and other gifts upon him enabling him to give frequent feasts and hold councils thus perpetuating the old
time customs amongst the Indians and engrafting with

their superstitious nature this additional absurdity of the "New Messiah" and "Return of the Ghosts" and in this coming, Sitting Bull whose former influence and power being so undermined and tenure so uncertain, asserts himself as "High Priest" here, and like a drowning man grasping at a straw is working upon the credulity of the superstitious and ignorant Indians and reaping a rich harvest of popularity, which with Mrs. Weldon's affection and numerous gifts he is doubtless self-satisfied.

On Thursday the 9th instant upon an invitation from Sitting Bull, an Indian named Kicking Bear, belonging to the Cheyenne River Agency, the Chief Medicine Man of the Ghost Dance among the Sioux, arrived at Sitting Bull's camp on Grand River, 40 miles south of this Agency to inaugurate a Ghost Dance and initiate the members. Upon learning of his arrival there I sent a detachment of 13 Policemen, including the Captain and Second Lieutenant, to arrest and escort him from the reservation, but they returned without executing the order, both officers being in a "dazed" condition and fearing the powers of Kicking Bear's medicine. Several members of the force tried to induce the officers to permit them to make the arrest but the latter would not allow it, simply told Sitting Bull that it was the Agent's orders that Kicking Bear and his six companions should leave the reservation and return to their Agency. Sitting Bull was very insolent to the officers and made some threats against certain members of the force but said that the visitors should leave the following day. Upon the return of the detachment to the Agency on Tuesday the 14th I immediately sent the Lieutenant and one man back to see whether the party had left or not and to notify Sitting Bull that his insolence and bad behavior would not be tolerated longer and that the "Ghost Dance" must not be continued. The Lieutenant returned yesterday and reported that the party had not started back to Cheyenne before his arrival there on the

morning of the 15th, but left immediately upon his ordering them to do so, and that Sitting Bull told him that he
was determined to continue the "'Ghost Dance" as the
Great Spirit had sent a direct message by Kicking Bear
that to live they must do so, but that he would not have
any more dancing until after he had come to the Agency
and talked the matter over with me, but the news comes
in this morning that they are dancing again and it is participated in by a great many Indians who become silly and
like men intoxicated over the excitement. The dance is
demoralizing, indecent and disgusting.

Desiring to exhaust all reasonable means before re-
sorting to extremes, I have sent a message to Sitting Bull
by his nephew One Bull that I want to see him at the
Agency and I feel quite confident that I shall succeed in
allaying the present excitement and put a stop to this absurd "craze" for the present at least, but I would respectfully recommend the removal from the reservation and
confinement in some Military prison some distance from
the Sioux country of Sitting Bull and the parties named
in my letter of June 18th last, hereinbefore referred to,
sometime during the coming winter and before next
spring opens. With these individuals removed the advancement of the Sioux will be more rapid and the interests of the Government greatly subserved thereby.

I am, Sir,

Very respectfully,

Your obd't. serv't.,

James McLaughlin,

U. S. Indian Agent.

Standing Rock Agency, N. D.,
November 19, 1890.

Hon. T. J. Morgan,

Commissioner of Indian Affairs, Washington, D. C.

Sir: Having just returned from Grand River District and referring to my former communication regarding the Ghost Dance Craze among the Indians, I have the honor to report that on Saturday evening last I learned that a dance was in progress in Sitting Bull's camp and that a large number of Indians of the Grand River settlements were participators. Sitting Bull's camp is on Grand River 40 miles southwest of Agency in a section of country outside of the line of travel, only visited by those connected with the Indian Service, and is therefore a secluded place for these séances.

I concluded to take them by surprise and on Sunday morning left for that settlement, accompanied by Louis Primeau, arriving there about three P. M., and having left the road usually traveled by me in visiting the settlement, got upon them unexpectedly and found a "Ghost Dance" at its height. There were about 45 men, 25 women, 25 boys and 10 girls participating, (a majority of the latter (boys and girls) were until a few weeks ago pupils of the day schools of the Grand River Settlements), and, approximately, 200 persons lookers on, who had come to witness the ceremony either from curiosity or sympathy, most of them having their families with them and encamped in the neighborhood.

I did not attempt to stop the dance then going on, as in their crazed condition under the excitement, it would have been useless to attempt it, but after remaining some time talking with a number of the spectators I went on to the house of Henry Bull Head, 3 miles distant, where I remained overnight, and returned to Sitting Bull's house early next morning where I had a long talk with Sitting Bull and a number of his followers. I spoke very plainly to them pointing out what had been done by the Government for the Sioux people and how this faction by their present conduct, were abusing the confidence that had been reposed in them by the Government in its magnanimity in granting them full amnesty for all past offenses when from destitution and imminent starvation they were compelled to surrender as prisoners of war in 1880 and 1881, and I dwelt at length upon what was being done in the way of education for their children and for their own industrial advancement and assured them of what this absurd craze would lead to and the chastisement that would certainly follow if these demoralizing dances and disregard of Department orders were not soon discontinued. I spoke with feeling and earnestness and my talk was well received and I am convinced that it had a good effect. Sitting Bull while being very obstinate and at first inclined to assume the role of "Big Chief" before his followers, finally admitted the truths of my reasoning and said that he believed me to be a friend to the Indians as a people but that I did not like him personally, but that when in doubt in any matter in following my advice he had always found it well, and that now he had a proposition to make to me which if I agreed to and would carry out would allay all further excitement among the Sioux over this Ghost Craze or else convince me of the truth of the belief of the Indians in this new doctrine. He then stated his proposition which was that I should accompany him on a journey to trace from this Agency to each of the other tribes of Indians through which the story of the Indian Messiah had been brought and when we reached the last tribe or where it originated if they could not produce the man who started the story and we did not find the New Messiah, as described, upon the earth, together with the dead Indians returning to re-inhabit this country he would return convinced that they (the Indians) had been too credulous and imposed upon, which report from him would satisfy the Sioux and all practices of the Ghost Societies would cease, but that if found to be as professed by the Indians they be permitted to continue their medicine practices and organize as they are now endeavoring to do.

I told him that his proposition was a novel one but that the attempt to carry it into effect would be similar to the attempt to catch the wind that blew last year, but that I wished him to come to my house where I would give him a whole night or day and night in which time I thought I could convince him of the absurdity of this foolish craze and the fact of his making me the proposition he did was a convincing proof that he did not fully believe in what he was professing and endeavoring so hard to make others believe. He did not however promise fully to come in to the Agency to discuss the matter but said he would consider my talk and decide after deliberation.

I consumed three days in making this trip and feel well repaid by what I accomplished, as my presence in their midst encouraged the weaker and doubting, and set those who are believers to thinking of the advisability of continuing the nonsensical practices they are now engaged in. I also found that the active members in the dance were not more than half the number of the earlier dancers and believe that it is losing ground among these Indians, and while there are many who are half-believers I am full satisfied that I can keep the dance confined to the Grand River District.

Desiring to use every reasonable means to bring Sitting Bull and his followers to abandon this dance and to look upon its practice as detrimental to their individual interests and the welfare of their children I made the trip herein reported to ascertain the extent of the disaffection and the best means of effecting its discontinuance. From close observation I am fully convinced that the dance can be broken up and after due reflection would respectfully suggest that, in case my visit to Sitting Bull fails to bring him in to see me in regard to the matter as invited to do, all Indians living on Grand River be notified that those wishing to be known as opposed to the Ghost Doctrine, friendly to the Government and desiring the support provided in the treaty must report at the Agency for such enrollment and be required to encamp near the Agency for a few weeks; and those electing to continue their medicine practices in violation of Department orders to remain on Grand River from whom subsistence issues will be withheld.

Something looking towards breaking up this craze should be done, and now, that cold weather is approaching, is the proper time. Such a step as here suggested would leave Sitting Bull with but few followers, as all or nearly all would soon report for enrollment and thus he would be forced in himself.

There are not many firearms among these Indians, still there are a few, and as a pledge of good faith on their part, they should be required to turn in all their arms to the Agent and get a memorandum receipt for the same. Knowing these Indians as I do I am confident that I can by such a course settle the Messiah craze at this Agency, and also thus break up the power of Sitting Bull without trouble and very little excitement; this will be sustained by public sentiment and conform to the discipline approved by the better disposed Indians. It is true that it would unsettle the Indians of that district in their home life for a few weeks but after which all worry and uneasiness would cease, while with the Ghost practices continued, all the participants being Indians regularly rationed by the Government without any appearance of withdrawal of this support, anxiety among the well disposed and the greater temptation for many others to join is increased.

A reply to the suggestion herein contained is respectfully requested

I am, Sir,

Very respectfully,

Your obd't. serv't.,
James McLaughlin,
U. S. Indian Agent.

(COPY TELEGRAM)
Fort Yates, N. D., November 21, 1890.
Commissioner of Indian Affairs, Washington, D. C.

Replying to Office telegram of yesterday, Sitting Bull, Circling Bear, Black Bird, Circling Hawk, Iron White Man, and Male Bear, being leaders of excitement and fomenters of disaffection should be removed before next spring, but everything being quiet here at present, with no snow and the weather summer-like, do not think it prudent to make arrests now. My letter of nineteenth suggests plan of settling matters and suppressing craze at this Agency.

McLaughlin,
Agent.

(COPY TELEGRAM)
Fort Yates, N. D., November 28, 1890.
Commissioner of Indian Affairs, Washington, D. C.

William F. Cody (Buffalo Bill) has arrived here with commission from General Miles to arrest Sitting Bull. Such a step at present is unnecessary and unwise as it will precipitate a fight which can be averted.

A few Indians still dancing but does not mean mischief at present. I have matters well in hand and when proper time arrives can arrest Sitting Bull by Indian police without bloodshed. I ask attention to my letter of November nineteenth (19th). Request General Miles' order to Cody be rescinded, and request immediate answer.

McLaughlin,
Agent.

(COPY TELEGRAM)

Fort Yates, N. D., November 29, 1890.

Commissioner of Indian Affairs, Washington, D. C.

Your telegram of this date contains the same information as to Cody's mission as the one received last night and is in the same words. Is there any mistake in transmitting same instead of Secretary's decision.

McLaughlin,

Agent.

Standing Rock Agency,

November 29, 1890.

Hon. T. J. Morgan,

Commissioner of Indian Affairs, Washington, D. C.

Sir:

I have the honor to acknowledge the receipt of Office letter "L," dated the 22nd instant directing me to keep the Office fully posted of the condition and temper of the Indians under my charge as to the prevailing excitement connected with the Ghost Dance. In reply I respectfully invite attention to my correspondence with the Department on the subject from which the following quotations are made.

My letter of October 17, 1890, states "I do not wish it to be understood as considering the present state of excitement so alarming as to apprehend any immediate uprising or serious outbreak." ... "it is undoubtedly a question of time only (a few months at the most) when it will be necessary to remove him (Sitting Bull) from among his people and I believe that if we can tide over the present craze without removing him from the reservation it will be necessary to deal with him in a summary manner as soon as the survey of this reservation commences," and in conclusion of that communication I recommend "the removal from the reservation and confinement in some

Military prison some distance from the Sioux country of Sitting Bull and the parties named in my letter of June 18th last, therein before referred to, sometime during the coming winter and before next spring opens."

The monthly report of this Agency dated November 15, informs the Department that the greater number of these Indians are loyal to the Government and the disaffected well in hand, and further that the excitement was subsiding at this Agency and that Sitting Bull could be arrested at any time by the Indian police when they were so ordered. This arrest I stated was not deemed advisable or necessary at the present time but that it should be carried into effect before next spring opened.

Later I visited the camp of Sitting Bull and witnessed the "dance" which I reported to the Office in letter of the 19th inst. and such report contains an account of my interview with Sitting Bull and its result. My views with regard to the dance are fully set forth in the report, as well as my conclusions that the craze was losing ground and would eventually die out. I also suggested a plan which it was proposed to adopt for securing this end.

In telegram of 21st inst. in reply to one from the Department I gave certain names of leaders in this excitement as the proper parties to be arrested before next spring, but that on account of the extremely fine weather I did not consider it prudent to make the arrests now.

I again telegraphed the Department yesterday protesting against the action of General Miles in ordering the arrest of Sitting Bull who I believe is the only party mentioned in his (General Miles') commission to Mr. Cody (Buffalo Bill) and stating that such a step at present was unnecessary and unwise.

I have quoted from these communications to show that my action in the premises from the first has been consistent, and also to show to what extent the orders and regulations of the Bureau are disobeyed by certain

Indians of this reservation, and also that fact of my never asking for military assistance in making arrests and my protest against military interference shall go on record.

I deplore the widespread reports appearing in the newspapers which are greatly and criminally exaggerated, and in a majority of instances without any truth whatever in so far as this Agency is concerned, for they have caused an unnecessary alarm amongst settlers in the vicinity who have fled from their homes, panic stricken to places of supposed safety, on false rumors that the Indians had broken out; the reports besides having the tendency to excite the Indians to hostility and disobedience of orders rather than to allay the excitement amongst them, and I feel quite confident the interference of the military at this time will result in resistance and possibly precipitate a fight and consequent bloodshed, for the weather is suitable to Indian hostilities while cold weather is not.

I have not, as questioned by the newspapers, lost control of my Indians and if the military do not interfere I yet feel competent to handle them and am confident of success in quelling the excitement at this Agency in case the Department authorizes me to adopt the plan I suggested in my letter of the 19th inst.; the adoption of this plan at the present time and the arrest by Indian police of Sitting Bull and others named, when the proper time arrives, will accomplish the end sought for, viz.: the disappearance of the "Ghost Dance," peace and safety in the vicinity of this reservation, and a recognition by Indians of the determination of the Government to punish evil doers and leaders of disaffection, encourage industrial pursuits and stimulate civilization.

While recognizing the importance of suppressing this craze and the punishment of all the leaders, which is necessary to encourage and protect all the well disposed Indians I, at the same time know that there are many now believing in the "Ghost Dance" who are ignorant and therefore dupes of the more cunning leaders, and while the conduct of some might seem to warrant the harsher measures still the milder course will be as salutary and in a short time bring many of the deluded to see the absurdity of this false doctrine, and thus brought to appreciate the magnanimity of the Government in tolerating for so long a time that which has had such a demoralizing effect for a time which tolerance was only to save bloodshed and loss of life of those ignorant fanatics who in their unenlightened state and with their inherent superstition fell easy victims of the more wily medicine men of the tribes.

After vainly trying to persuade Cody to wait here for the instructions which I was expecting from Washington and against my earnest protest, he (Cody) with 8 civilian companions, and no other escort left the Agency and post today at 11 A. M., for the purpose of going to Sitting Bull's camp.

I am, Sir,

Very respectfully,

Your obd't. serv't.,

James McLaughlin,

U. S. Indian Agent.

Standing Rock Agency,

December 1, 1890.

Hon. T. J. Morgan,

Commissioner of Indian Affairs, Washington, D. C.

Sir:

Referring to that part of my letter of the 29th instant which contains the information that Cody (Buffalo Bill) had left for Sitting Bull's camp, I have the honor to state that four hours after his departure a dispatch was received at the military post from Army Headquarters directing the suspension of the arrest of Sitting Bull, and other Indians and couriers were at once sent out after Cody to notify him of the fact. These couriers failed to fall in with Cody, but the latter was met on the road by some citizens who were coming to the Agency and they informed him that Sitting Bull was on his way to have a council with the Agent.

Cody returned to camp about four miles distant from the post where a copy of the dispatch was sent to him. Cody and party left for the east yesterday. Sitting Bull has thus far failed to make an appearance as we were led to believe by the citizens above referred to.

I am waiting for the weather to change when I intend to arrest Sitting Bull by the Indian police and will report promptly any changes in this respect in affairs at this Agency.

I am, Sir,

Very respectfully,

Your obd't. serv't.,

James McLaughlin,

U. S. Indian Agent.

(COPY TELEGRAM)

Fort Yates, N. D., December 4, 1890.

Commissioner of Indian Affairs, Washington, D. C.

Everything quiet at present. Weather cold and snowing. Am I authorized to arrest Sitting Bull and other fomentors of mischief when I think best?

McLaughlin,

Agent.

(COPY TELEGRAM)

Standing Rock Agency,

Fort Yates, N. D., December 6, 1890.

To General Ruger,

St. Paul, Minn.

No change in condition except for the better. Sitting Bull can be kept on reserve by Indian Police without fear of escape before arrest is required; which can be made by Indian Police, but in my judgment there is no necessity for immediate arrest, postponement preferable as every day of cold weather cools the ardor of the dancers. This is beef ration day and everything is quiet.

McLaughlin,

Agent.

(COPY TELEGRAM)

Fort Yates, N. D., December 15, 1890.

Commissioner of Indian Affairs, Washington, D. C.

Indian police arrested Sitting Bull at his camp forty miles southwest of Agency at day light this morning. His followers attempted his rescue and fighting commenced. Four policemen killed and three wounded. Eight Indians killed including "Sitting Bull" and his son "Crow Foot" and several others wounded. Police were surrounded for some time but maintained their ground until relieved by U. S. troops, who now have possession of Sitting Bull's camp with all women, children and property. Sitting Bull's followers, probably one hundred men, deserted their families and fled west up Grand River

Police behaved nobly, and great credit is due them.

Particulars by mail.

McLaughlin,

Agent.

Standing Rock Agency, December 16, 1890.

Hon. T. J. Morgan,

Commissioner of Indian Affairs, Washington, D. C.

Sir:

In accordance with my telegram of yesterday inform-
ing you of a fight with the Indians of this reservation I
now have the honor to make the following detailed statement. My action in the matter has been governed by
Department instructions.

The troops left Fort Yates at 12 P. M., on the night of
Sunday the 14th instant for Grand River, with Louis
Primeau as Guide, and my Indian Police who were then
at Grand River, or en route, were instructed to arrest Sitting Bull when the troops were sufficiently near to afford
them protection in case of resistance to the arrest.

At day break on Monday morning the 15th the police
went to Sitting Bull's camp direct to his house and surrounded the house; a detail was sent into the house where
Sitting Bull was sleeping on the floor, the remainder stay-
ing outside. They aroused him and announced their purpose, at the same time raising him to a sitting position,
and he at first seemed to offer no resistance and they allowed him to dress, during which time he changed his
mind and they took him forcibly from the house. By this
time the police were surrounded by Sitting Bull's followers, members of the Ghost Dance, and the first shot was
fired by "Catch the Bear," one of the hostiles and the Lieutenant of Police, Henry Tatankapah, (Bull Head), who was
in command of the detachment of 42 men, was struck;
the fighting then became general, in fact it was a hand to
hand fight. Sitting Bull was killed, shot through the body
and head in the early part of the fight by Bull Head and
Marcelus Chankpidutah (Red Tomahawk), who each shot
at him. Four policemen were killed outright and three
wounded, one of the latter dying at the Agency Hospital
this morning after his removal there.

Bull Head, the Lieutenant of Police, is dangerously
wounded but may recover. The hostile Indians lost 8 killed
and several wounded and were driven from the field by
the police; they fled up Grand River, leaving their wives
and families and all their property and dead behind them.

Two troops of the U. S. Cavalry (100 men) arrived on the ground immediately after the fight which had occupied less than half an hour and took possession of the camp, its inhabitants, property and dead.

The military did not pursue the fleeing hostile and the latter will no doubt fall into the hands of someone of the commands moving at the different points west or south of the reservation.

The Police returned about 3 P. M. today accompanied by the Cavalry detachment having charge of the remains of the four dead policemen and Sitting Bull, also two prisoners, Henry Growler, Sitting Bull's nephew, 21 years old, and Middle, son of Little Assinaboine, 21 years old.

The dead Policemen will be buried tomorrow at the Agency with military honors. Sitting Bull's remains are in possession of the military at Fort Yates.

The details of the battle show that the Indian Police behaved nobly and exhibited the best of judgment and bravery, and a recognition by the Government for their services on this occasion is richly deserved and should be promptly given with a substantial allowance for the families of those who are dead and also for the survivors to show them that the Government recognizes the great service that has been done for the country in the result of yesterday's fight.

I respectfully urge that the Interior Department cooperate with the War Department in obtaining Congressional action which will secure to these brave survivors and to the families of the dead a full and generous reward. Besides the Indian police there were four volunteers, viz: "Gray Eagle," "Spotted Thunder," "Otter Robe," and "Young Eagle," who participated in the fight rendering good service and deserving like recognition. Gray Eagle (Gabriel Wamblihotah), is one of the Judges of the Court of Indian Offenses, and his two sisters are Sitting Bull's wives; until about 17 months ago he was Sitting Bull's main support.

CASUALTIES IN THE POLICE FORCE

Henry Tatankapah (Bull Head), First Lieutenant, in command, dangerously wounded, 4 wounds.

Charles Kashlah (Shave Head), First Sergeant, mortally wounded, since dead.

James Wambdichigalah (Little Eagle), Fourth Sergeant, killed.

Alexander Hocokah (Middle), Private, painfully wounded.

Paul Akichitah (Afraid of Soldier), Private, killed.

John Armstrong, Special Police, killed.

Hawk Man, Special Police, killed.

Indians killed outright and bodies held by police:

1—Sitting Bull.

2—Black Bird, very bad man.

3—Catch the Bear, very bad man.

4—Little Assinaboine, very bad man.

5—Crow Foot (Sitting Bull's son, 17 years old, a bad young man).

6—Spotted Horn Bull, a chief.

7—Brave Thunder, a chief.

8—Chase Wounded.

and several others wounded but carried off by their friends and whose names are not yet known.

A large majority of the Indians of this Agency are loyal to the Government and universal satisfaction is expressed by them as it ends the Ghost Craze here.

I have sent couriers to overtake the fleeing Indians advising them to return as their only safety was at the Agency, and if found outside of the Reservation they must suffer the consequences.

While this conflict causing the loss of some of our best, (*noble and brave*) policemen is to be very much regretted, yet the great good accomplished by the ending of Sitting Bull's career, whose influence has been of such a retarding nature, and the determination the police manifested in maintaining the will of the Government, is most gratifying.

I enclose copies of telegrams showing the authority under which the Indian Police were engaged in the arrest of Sitting Bull, also copy of a message sent in by John M. Carignan, Teacher of the Grand River Day School, showing the contemplated flight of Sitting Bull, and the necessity for his immediate arrest, also a rough sketch of the battleground.

I am, Sir,

Very respectfully,

Your obd't. serv't.,

James McLaughlin,

U. S. Indian Agent.

5 Inclosures.

Standing Rock Agency, December 19, 1890.

Hon. T. J. Morgan,

Commissioner of Indian Affairs, Washington, D. C.

Sir:

Referring to my letter of the 16th instant, I regret to have to report that First Lieutenant Henry Tatankapah (Bull Head), of the Indian Police, who was reported dangerously wounded in the engagement on the Grand River on the morning of the 15th inst., died last evening at 4 P. M., at the Agency Hospital, from the effects of his wounds, making a total of 6 Indian police who lost their lives in the fight.

I am, Sir,

Very respectfully,

Your obd't. serv't.,

James McLaughlin,

U. S. Indian Agent.

194, L. P., D. D., 1890.

HEADQUARTERS DEPARTMENT OF DAKOTA
St. Paul, Minn., December 17, 1890.
Major James McLaughlin, U. S. Indian Agent,
Through Commanding Officer Fort Yates, N. D.
Sir:

Referring to telegram of this date from the Commanding Officer, Fort Yates, recommending that some recognition and reward should be bestowed on your Indian police for their fidelity and bearing in the arrest of Sitting Bull and the consequent encounter with his followers; it will give me pleasure to unite with you in promoting any recommendation you may make for suitable reward to those who are entitled, and provision for the families of those who were killed.

Very respectfully,
Your obedient servant,
(*Signed*) Thos. H. Ruger,
Brigadier General, Commanding.

STANDING ROCK AGENCY
Fort Yates, N. D., December 22, 1890.
General T. H. Ruger,
Commanding the Dept. of Dakota, St. Paul, Minn.
General:

I have the honor to acknowledge receipt of your letter of the 17th instant by which you kindly offer to unite in promoting any recommendation for suitable reward to the survivors of the police force in the Grand River fight on the 15th instant, and for provision for the families of the killed. I am very glad to receive this offer, as it shows that the service rendered by the police is recognized by the Department Commander and that he considers a reward merited. I shall feel grateful for any suggestions which may assist in promoting the object in question.

I have already represented the matter to the Indian Office with a request that the co-operation of the War

Department be secured; I have also furnished to Senator G. A. Pierce, of North Dakota, a full account of the affair (with a copy of the Department Commander's letter of the 17th instant), with a view to obtaining his action in presenting and supporting a bill in Congress. In the meantime I shall be glad to receive your support in what has already been done, by any special representation to the War Department or otherwise as may be deemed best and to act upon any suggestion which you think advisable to make and also to furnish any information that may be needed, and in my power to furnish, which is not already in the hands of the military authorities.

I am, Sir,

Very respectfully,

Your obd't. serv't.,

James McLaughlin,

U. S. Indian Agent.

(COPY TELEGRAM)

Fort Yates, N. D., December 30, 1890.

Hon. Secretary of the Interior,

Washington, D. C.

The Division Commander's order, received on the twelfth (12th) instant, by telegram, to the Post Commander at Fort Yates, directs the latter to "make it his especial duty to secure the person of Sitting Bull and call on the Indian Agent to co-operate and render such assistance as would best promote the purpose in view."

After receipt of this telegram a consultation was held between the Post Commander and myself when it was decided that the arrest be made on the twentieth (20th) instant when most of the Indians of Sitting Bull's camp would be absent from there, receiving their rations at Agency. Information reached me on the evening of the fourteenth (14th) that Sitting Bull was preparing to leave the reservation, which I reported to the Post Commander who ordered the arrest made at once, and it was arranged to send the police to the camp for that purpose, and for the troops to leave the post and reach their destination in time to prevent a rescue. Under my instructions to co-operate with the military, and in pursuance of the arrangement between the Post Commander and myself, I issued the order to the police.

My action was governed by previous telegraphic instructions of December first (1) and fifth (5th) from the Indian Office directing me to co-operate with the military.

Full details, with copies of orders and instructions, have heretofore been forwarded to Indian Office, but I will send copies, if required, as soon as they can be prepared.

The body of Sitting Bull was brought to this Agency by the troops and is buried in the Fort Yates Military Cemetery.

James McLaughlin,
U. S. Indian Agent.

Standing Rock Agency, January 7, 1891.
Hon. T. J. Morgan,
Commissioner of Indian Affairs, Washington, D. C.
Sir:

I desire respectfully to state, for the information that, in contradiction of the absurd statements appearing from time to time in the public press, there has been no trouble or disaffection amongst the Indians of this reservation since the affair of the 15th on the Grand River.

The Grand River Indians, or such as remain of them, are peaceably encamped near the Agency waiting for permission to return to the settlement, and a feeling of quiet and safety is universal amongst all Indians on this reservation, which can be verified by the Post Commander of Fort Yates and other officers of the Army present at the post or in the vicinity.

I am, Sir,
Very respectfully,
Your obd't. serv't.,
James McLaughlin,
U. S. Indian Agent.

(COPY TELEGRAM)

Fort Yates, N. D., January 9, 1891.
Commissioner of Indian Affairs, Washington, D. C.

Reports of Indians leaving this reservation entirely unfounded. None have left since the Sitting Bull affair. Three hundred and seventy-two (372) men, women and children now absent, of whom two hundred and twenty-seven (227) are prisoners at Fort Sully and on third (3rd) instant General Miles telegraphed the Post Commander here that seventy-two (72) Standing Rock Indians were made prisoners at Pine Ridge Agency, which leaves only seventy-three (73) unaccounted for of whom forty (40) were absent before the stampede of fifteenth (15th) ultimo.

Newspaper reports that Indians here are restless and unsettled ridiculously absurd. Standing Rock Indians are under excellent control, loyal to the Government and can be depended upon to remain so, as all disaffection has been effectually eradicated with the departure and subjugation of Sitting Bull's followers. The Department may depend on my keeping it correctly and promptly informed of any important facts.

McLaughlin,
Agent.

Standing Rock Agency, January 23, 1891.
Hon. T. J. Morgan,
Commissioner of Indian Affairs, Washington, D. C.
Sir:

I have the honor to acknowledge receipt of your communication of January 12, 1891, L. 26, 1891, in which, referring to my report of December 24, 1890, it is stated that the authority under which I co-operated and the Indian police acted in the matter of the capture and killing of Sitting Bull on the 15th of December last, is not directly stated and specifically set out, and calling for further report in this particular.

I invite a perusal of the concluding paragraph of my report of December 16, in which I state that copies if telegrams showing authority under which the Indian police were engaged in the arrest of Sitting Bull were enclosed. These copies consist as follows:

1. Office telegram of December 1, in which the following order appears, "You will as to the operations intended to suppress any outbreak by force co-operate with and obey the orders of the military officers commanding on the reservation in your charge."

2. Office telegram of December 5 states: "Replying to your telegram of this date Secretary directs that you make no arrests whatever except under orders of the military or upon an order of the Secretary of the Interior."

3. Telegram dated December 12, from General Ruger, Commanding the Military Department of Dakota, to Colonel W. F. Drum, Commanding Officer, Fort Yates, which is in the following words: "The Division Commander has directed that you make it your especial duty to secure the person of Sitting Bull. Call on Indian Agent to co-operate and render such assistance as will best promote the purpose in view."

Upon receipt of the letter written for Bull Head by John M. Carignan, Teacher of the Grand River Day School, dated December 14, 1890, 12:30 A. M., a copy of which was furnished with my report of December 16, 1890, Lieut. Col. W. F. Drum, U. S. A., Commanding Fort Yates, ordered the arrest, and acting under previous instructions to co-operate I issued the orders to the Indian police directing them to proceed to Sitting Bull's camp and make the arrest the following morning and bring him in towards the Agency until they met the troops to which command they were to deliver the prisoner or, escorted by the military bring him through to the post of Fort Yates, as might be determined by the officer commanding the detachment of troops. The orders to the police referred to above is in the following words:

(*Translation from the Sioux*)

Standing Rock Agency, N. D., December 14, 1890. Afraid of Bear and Shave Head:

I am in receipt of the letter you sent by courier Hawkman, and I have come to the conclusion that the time has come to arrest Sitting Bull. I am afraid that if we should put it off any longer that he will get away from us, so, tonight you will proceed to his house and arrest him before daybreak. Louie will lead the troops down on the road you suggested, to Oak Creek Crossing and stop there. I mean the Sitting Bull and Spotted Horn Bull Crossing of Oak Creek, where I told you to build the station and they will await you there. If anything should happen you will bring the news to the troops immediately.

I am your Agent,

James McLaughlin.

("Afraid of Bear" is the same person referred to in the affair as Bull Head and the letter referred to as sent by courier is the one written for Bull Head and signed by John M. Carignan hereinbefore referred to).

All preliminary orders given by me to the police were verbal as well as the orders from Colonel Drum to me; the plan of the arrest together with the disposition of the police and troops was decided upon in consultation, both of us concurring, after a joint, careful study of the situation.

I do not see that I can further improve my reports of December 16 and 24, so as to make more clear the nature of the orders under which I and the police acted in this matter. It was in co-operation with the military who had determined upon the arrest of Sitting Bull, and in pursuance of Colonel Drum's direct verbal orders, that I gave all final orders to the police who were in this case what may be termed concomitants of the military.

I invite attention to that part of my report of December 24 commencing at page 6 which details all the preparations made as far as I was concerned with the full knowledge and by previous arrangement with the Post Commander and under his instructions.

I submit enclosed copies of correspondence with the Honorable Secretary for the Interior for the information of the Honorable Commissioner.

I am, Sir,

Very respectfully,

Your obd't. serv't.,

James McLaughlin,

U. S. Indian Agent.

Endorsements upon the papers of which the following are copies:

NATIONAL INDIAN DEFENSE ASSOCIATION

1121 Tenth Street, N. W.

Washington, D. C., December 27, 1890.

To the Hon. Commissioner of Indian Affairs.

Sir:

I observe in the public press a statement to the effect that the body of Sitting Bull was removed from the coffin, before it was buried, and taken to a dissecting room. The reasonable supposition is: that it is the intention of the parties having the matter in charge to make his bones a subject of speculation and perhaps his skin also, as the papers state that a Bismarck merchant offered $1,000 for it. I beg to ask if you do not hold it the duty of the Government, as the guardian of the Indians, to inquire into this matter and take measures to punish any parties, whether Government official or not, who may be found guilty of such desecration of the dead chief's body.

Respectfully,

(Signed) T. A. Bland.

L 40319-1890.

DEPARTMENT OF THE INTERIOR
Office of Indian Affairs
Washington, January 12, 1891.

James McLaughlin, Esq.,
U. S. Indian Agent,
Standing Rock Agency, N. D.

Sir:

I transmit herewith for investigation and report letter from Dr. T. A. Bland dated the 27th ultimo, relative to reports that the body of Sitting Bull was removed from the coffin before burial and taken to a dissecting room, etc.

You will return the letter with your report.

Very respectfully,

T. J. Morgan,
Commissioner.

1ST ENDORSEMENT
Standing Rock Agency, Fort Yates, N. D.,
January 23, 1891.

As the body of Sitting Bull was taken to the Military Post of Fort Yates upon its arrival from Grand River, this paper is respectfully referred to the Commanding Officer of Fort Yates, for such information and remarks as he may be pleased to make concerning the matter to assist me in replying to the Commissioner's letter.

James McLaughlin,

U. S. Indian Agent.

3RD ENDORSEMENT

Post Hospital, Fort Yates, N. D.,

January 23, 1891.

Respectfully returned to the Post Adjutant. I received the body of Sitting Bull about 4:30 P. M., on the 16th of December, 1890, and it was in my custody until it was buried on the 17th. During that time it was not mutilated or disfigured in any manner. I saw the body, sewed up in canvas put in a coffin and the lid screwed down and afterwards buried in the N. W. corner of the Post Cemetery, in a grave about 8 feet deep—in the presence of Capt. A. R. Chapin, Assistant Surgeon, U. S. A.; Lieut. P. G. Wood, 12th Infantry, Post Quartermaster, and myself.

H. M. Deeble,

A. A. Surgeon, U. S. A., Post Surgeon.

4TH ENDORSEMENT

Fort Yates, N. D.,

January 24, 1891.

Respectfully returned to Indian Agent James McLaughlin, inviting attention to 3rd Endorsement hereon. The grave does not appear to have been disturbed.

W. F. Drum,

Lt. Col. 12th Infty., Commdg. Post.

5TH ENDORSEMENT

January 27, 1891.

Respectfully returned to the Honorable Commissioner of Indian Affairs, inviting attention to the endorsements of the Acting Assistant Surgeon and Commanding Officer of Fort Yates.

The body of Sitting Bull, together with the dead policemen, was brought to the Agency in the afternoon of the 16th by the police (who were acting under the direction of the military) whence, after depositing the dead policemen it (Sitting Bull's body), was taken at once by the police without removal from the wagon in which it was brought from Grand River, to the post of Fort Yates and there left in charge of the military authorities in pursuance of the Division Commander's orders to the Post Commander, before the arrest directing the latter to secure the person of Sitting Bull.

I saw Sitting Bull's remains upon arrival at Agency and was present on the afternoon of December 17th, 1890, in the Military Cemetery and saw his grave which had been partly filled with soil before I got there, and feel confident that he was neither dissected or scalped before burial and also quite confident that his grave has not been disturbed since.

James McLaughlin,
U. S. Indian Agent.

Standing Rock Agency, February 4, 1891.
Hon. T. J. Morgan,
Commissioner of Indian Affairs, Washington, D. C.
Sir:

I have the honor to state that on January 31st, last, I received a copy of General Orders No. 2, Headqrs. Mil. Div. of the Mo., in the Field, dated January 12, 1891, assigning certain Military Officers to duty at the several Sioux and Cheyenne Indian Agencies but *not* including Standing Rock; and today I have received a copy of

General Orders No. 2, from the same Headquarters, dated at Chicago, January 30, paragraphs II and III of which give the same powers to Lieutenant Colonel Drum, 12th Infantry, with regard to Standing Rock Agency, as are conferred on other Military officers at the Agencies named in the order of January 12.

I strongly protest against the requirements of paragraphs II and III of the order of January 30, embracing as they do the provisions of paragraphs 5, 6, 7, and 8 of the order of January 12, which suggest the question: "What has occurred since January 12 in the management of this Agency that should serve as a pretext to General Miles for extending the provisions of the order of that date so as to include the Standing Rock Agency?"

In the interests of peace, in justice to myself, and to prevent serious trouble which I foresee will arise from conflict of authority, I most earnestly and respectfully request that the Indian Bureau take the proper steps to cause the revocation of the order of January 30, so far as relates to this Agency. On reading this order of January 30 it might be inferred that the paragraph III originated with General Miles and did not form part of his original recommendation approved by the Honorable Secretary of War as recited in paragraph 2.

In the future, as in the past, I feel fully competent to manage this reservation and. agency without the interference of any supervising power present at the Agency, and not withstanding all the temptation held out by the action of General Miles by what I consider unnecessary precipitation during the recent troubles I kept the majority of my Indians in subjection and retained them on their reservation.

I have been in the Government service amongst the Indians for twenty consecutive years, and been Agent for the Sioux for 15 years last past.

I am a bonded officer under which I am responsible to the Government and my Commission gives me full control of these Indians and the reservation under the orders of the proper Department and in the absence of any just cause I protest against my authority being thus interfered with as the unlimited powers given to officers of another Department will certainly lessen my influence as Agent over the Indians and cannot be otherwise than detrimental to the service.

I am about to reorganize such of the reservation schools as were discontinued on account of the late disturbance:—the Indians of the Grand River settlements who were called to the Agency by me and have been kept here since December 15, to defeat any attempts to bring them into trouble by trying to make it appear that the Indians were leaving the reservation to join the hostiles, (but this precaution was not sufficient to prevent unprincipled men from conveying such impressions to the public), also to prevent any uneasiness or trouble that might arise from the movements of troops from place to place in that section of country, have returned to their homes; the troops have returned to the post from duty outside the reservation; the chief conspirator in the disaffection has been removed and everything is quiet and peaceable on the reservation. I do not hesitate to assert confidently that this peace will continue unless interrupted by the interference of the military and the conflict of authority which will necessarily follow the operation of General Miles' order.

It is well enough to maintain military posts which are as much needed in a civilized community as amongst Indians, but as a factor in the civilization of the Indians the rank and file of the Army is a failure, on the contrary their presence in an Indian community is baneful and conducive to demoralization.

To sum up, I protest in a general way against the aggressive policy of General Miles in seeking to obtain control of all Indian Agencies, and I desire to be understood that my protest is made on general principles looking to

the advancement, good government and ultimate civilization of Indians and not on personal grounds.

With regard to the officer designated for the duty at
this Agency I desire to state that I have every confidence
in the sound sense and good judgment of Lieutenant Colonel Drum, in this as in all other matters entrusted to him,
and I do not think anything would occur in the administration of Agency affairs under the Military Supervision
of that officer that would cause any conflict of authority
or be detrimental to the service or cause any dissatisfaction amongst the Indians, but changes in Post Command-
ers occur so frequently that Colonel Drum, the present
Commander of Fort Yates, may at any time be transferred
to some other post and an officer specially selected by
General Miles sent here to assume command, and any
officer exercising the powers contemplated in the order,
with General Miles' aggressive views in this respect could
not be otherwise than detrimental to the welfare of the
Indians and the inevitable result will follow.

An Indian Agent to be of most service to the Government must command the respect and confidence of his
Indians and by having any person of an arrogant disposition occupying the position contemplated by General
Miles' orders, it would soon belittle the Agent in the esti-
mation of the Indians and breed distrust. The Indians
must feel that their Agent possess intelligence and integ-
rity equal at least to any others associated with him and
with this confidence once shaken his usefulness to the
Government as an Agent for them is gone.

In conclusion I would ask the Honorable Commissioner to give his special consideration to the wording of
General Miles' orders and I would respectfully suggest
that in the words "*without interfering unnecessarily,
etc.,*" there is a world of meaning which can be construed
to meet any circumstances and justify any action of the
Military in connection with the control to which it has
been assigned.

I enclose copies of the Orders herein referred to which I respectfully request may be returned to me.

I am, Sir,

Very respectfully,

Your obd't. serv't.,

James McLaughlin,

U. S. Indian Agent.

Standing Rock Agency, February 18, 1891.

Hon. T. J. Morgan,

Commissioner of Indian Affairs, Washington, D. C.

Sir:

I have the honor to acknowledge receipt of your letter of November 29, 1890, L., calling for report with respect to a statement said to have been made by Sitting Bull that 1500 stand of arms were concealed near old Fort Stevenson for use by the Indians in case of an outbreak.

In the press of business, and the report being so absurd, the communication was laid aside for attention, an immediate, or if any reply, not being considered necessary.

I now desire to state that there is and was no foundation for any such report and I do not believe Sitting Bull would ever make such a statement for had there been any such concealment of arms Sitting Bull was too wily to divulge the secret.

After the Custer expedition in 1876 Sitting Bull and his followers fled to Canada and every description of fire arm which was then in their possession was disposed off in Canada to obtain necessary food for their subsistence before the surrender in 1880 and 1881, so that it was impossible with the means they have had since to accumulate the number of arms reported to have been concealed.

I am, Sir,

Very respectfully,

Your obd't. serv't.,

James McLaughlin,
U. S. Indian Agent.

Standing Rock Agency, March 3, 1891.
Hon. T. J. Morgan,
    Commissioner of Indian Affairs, Washington, D. C.
Sir:
    I have the honor to enclose herewith papers, which
as the endorsements indicate, were intended to be handed
to U. S. Senator Pierce of North Dakota for the purpose
stated in the endorsements but owing to the adverse criti-
cisms of the press of the country which was ignorant of
the facts, the papers were withheld and not given to Senator Pierce at the time, and since his defeat for re-election
as Senator and it being so near the end of the session of
which he is a member it was considered useless to do so,
I therefore send them to the Department where they may
be of some assistance in obtaining relief for the Indian
police.
    I would respectfully suggest that a pension of at least
$15.00 per month be given the families of Lieutenant
Henry Bull Head and Sergeants Charles Shave Head and
James Little Eagle and $10.00 per month to families of
Privates Paul Akicitah, Hawkman No. 1, and John Armstrong who were killed in the engagement and to
Alexander Middle who was severely wounded and who will
probably yet lose his foot as he is still confined in hospital and recovery very doubtful; also that each of the 33
policemen and 4 volunteers, survivors of the engagement,
receive a medal commemorative of their fidelity, and pay-
ment at the rate of $50.00 per head for the ponies they
had killed and those that stampeded during the fight
which latter were subsequently picked up and taken off
by the Indians opposed to them who fled from the reservation at that time.

I am, Sir,

Very respectfully,

Your obd't serv't.,

   James McLaughlin,

      U. S. Indian Agent.

                Standing Rock Agency, March 6, 1891.

Hon. T. J. Morgan,

   Commissioner of Indian Affairs, Washington, D. C.

Sir:

   I have the honor to acknowledge receipt of Officer Letter dated the 19th ultimo, inclosing copy of a letter from Honorable Lyman R. Casey, U. S. Senator, dated February 14, 1891, suggesting that the Indian Bureau take the necessary steps to come into possession of as large a part of the personal effects of the late "Sitting Bull," the Indian Chief, as shall prove to be practicable and that if possession of such is obtained, use of them to the State of North Dakota for exhibition at the World's Fair to be permitted. I am directed to look into the matter, see what there may be of value or interest and how much it will cost to secure possession of them for the purpose indicated by Senator Casey.

   In reply I desire to state that Sitting Bull was not possessed of much property that would be of interest other than his Winchester rifle, redstone pipe, riding saddle, a few articles of clothing and possibly two horses that were usually rode or driven by him; his log cabin has also been spoken of as desirable property to secure for exhibition at the World's Fair.

   I would ask, is it advisable at this time that the friendly and well disposed Indians should see such prominence given to the memory of one who, during his life time, was a fomentor of mischief and a disaffected leader. There is no room for doubt but that the more recognition the progressive Indians receive for their conduct and example and the less notice shown obstructionists who advocate the old Indian life, the more will civilization be advanced among them.

Numerous small articles formerly the property of Sitting Bull, such as pipes, moccasins, articles of clothing, etc., have already been purchased from members of the Sitting Bull family, by persons who procured them through curiosity, and the intrinsic value of everything of this kind that he possessed other than the importance in which they may be held by the respective purchasers as relics, is very trifling.

I can readily procure for a reasonable consideration any of Sitting Bull's personal effects yet in possession of his family, including his log cabin if deemed advisable, but if this cabin should be desired by the World's Fair, I would suggest that it be purchased and exhibited not because it was Sitting Bull's house, but because it was at this building that the Indian police as officers of law and order made such a gallant and determined stand in upholding the Government against their own race and kindred on the morning of December 15, 1890.

The articles that have already been disposed of (some of which have been sent to friends of the purchasers in different parts of the country) will be more difficult to obtain than what the family may yet possess, but if desired all can doubtless be traced and recovered, but in making such collection it would require prudence, for should it become known that Sitting Bull's effects were being procured for purposes of public exhibition on account of the name and prominence of the former owner as a leader of disaffection, the non-progressive Indians would be highly elated and the progressive and well disposed correspondingly discouraged.

I would respectfully request to be advised as to the kind and quantity of effects desired and I will then be better able to judge as to best means of procuring them should it be so authorized by the Department.

I am, Sir,

Very respectfully,

Your obd't. serv't.,

James McLaughlin,

U. S. Indian Agent.

Standing Rock Agency, March 10, 1891.

Hon. T. J. Morgan,

Commissioner of Indian Affairs, Washington, D. C.

Sir:

I have the honor to acknowledge the receipt of your letter dated the 24th ultimo, relative to rumors of various kinds that reach your Office regarding a possibility of renewal of trouble among the Sioux at no distant day, and directing me to report upon certain points.

In reply I respectfully submit the following:

First. As to the real causes of the late outbreak I have to say that there were a number of causes any of which in itself would be insufficient and of little force, but united were sufficient to produce the recent troubles.

In the autumn of 1888 Measles broke out among the Indians and was epidemic at all the Sioux Agencies throughout the following winter. "LeGrippe" and "Whooping Cough" followed in the winter of 1889 and '90 and an unusual number of deaths resulted.

The severe drouths rendered all efforts of Agriculture a failure for the past three years and many of the Indians' stock cattle died of black-leg.

Through the liberal aid by Government for bettering the condition of the Indians and the wise policy pursued by the Department in fostering education and industrial pursuits together with the missionary work of the several Christian organizations, civilization was steadily advancing among the Indians. This advancement was stubbornly opposed by the old time Chiefs and Medicine Men, who, on account of the new ways and better order of things, were steadily losing their power, and this class of Indians clinging tenaciously to the old Indian life encouraged by their non-progressive followers were those who strenuously opposed the ratification of the Act of March 2d, 1889; the delay by Government in making good the promises of that Commission together with the fact that whites commenced settling upon the lands enabled this element to taunt the signers with having ratified the Act of Congress ceding the large tract without receiving the compensation promised, and these taunts augmented disaffection and counteracted the civilization engrafted amongst the Indians.

There has been much said about scarcity of food being the chief cause of the late troubles, but in so far as the Indians of this Agency were concerned the contrary would be more tenable for the reason that the certainty of the subsistence issued at regular intervals, left it unnecessary for them to augment the ration by their own industry and the disaffected element had therefore ample time to brood over imaginary wrongs and the decimation of their race. The failure of crops again last summer, added to their other grievances, found then in a frame of mind ready to accept the absurd "Messiah" doctrine, which reached the Sioux about that time whereby the shrewd Medicine Men saw an opportunity to recover prestige and former popularity by uniting all in a common belief, added to which were the many absurd and sensational newspaper reports which alarmed frontier settlers and the public generally, causing additional troops to be sent into the Indian country and which with its active movements and the unlimited powers that were given the Military in these operations alarmed the Indians very much and enabled the wily leaders to organize in better shape all the disaffected and more ignorant of the several bands of Sioux in what they were made to believe was common cause and their own safety. I do not believe that any such considerable number of the Sioux could ever have been united in organized force opposed to the Government were it not that the inherent superstition of the average Indian is such that many of them at that time were victims of a religious frenzy through which they were drawn into what they would not have voluntarily joined.

Second. The causes which produced the former outbreak, in so far as the Indians of this Agency are concerned, have been removed by the death of "Sitting Bull," who was the chief leader of disaffection here, together with the fact that the Ghost doctrine has been effectually eradicated at this Agency and that the progressive and well disposed Indians have full confidence that the Government will carry out all promises made by the Crook Commission. There are only two men here of any prominence ("Thunder Hawk" and "Running Antelope"), who were admirers and supporters of Sitting Bull, but they have few followers and would never take a stand in opposition to the will of the Government. Another sub-chief named Red Fish, a Lower Yanktonais Sioux, is a chronic grumbler and is always applying for transfer to some other Agency or permission to locate east of the Missouri off the reservation, but he is harmless except his nonsensical talk and no trouble need be feared from him.

I have always kept the Indians under my charge informed upon all legislation bearing upon Indian matters as soon as I was fully informed myself, but have never thought it advisable to report to them newspaper articles touching on such until I had something more definite and reliable.

I have, however, notified them of the legislation recently enacted by Congress necessary to make good the promises of the Crook Commission, although I have not yet received any copy of the recent Acts relating to same but saw by the public press that such had become law, and as soon as I receive a copy of these Acts of Congress with the synopsis of the specific agreements in them, referred to in your letter of February 24, which were *not* inclosed as therein stated but which I have written for today, I will call the Indians together as directed and explain the whole matter fully to them.

Third. As to what in my judgment has been the general effect upon the minds of the Indians of this Agency of the recent occurrences I would state that while sorrow over the shedding of blood and loss of life is generally felt and regretted, yet universal satisfaction is expressed at the settlement of the trouble even at that cost, and a feeling of contentment is manifest amongst all the Indians now here.

Fourth. So far as I can observe or ascertain there are no indications of growing discontent or any danger to be apprehended of future trouble at this Agency and if common sense is exercised in their management and they are not frightened into trouble by unnecessary military movements among them no fear of further trouble may be entertained.

Fifth. To insure peace and quiet upon the several reservations I would respectfully recommend the disarming of all the Sioux, and I am of the opinion that this could be carried into effect without much difficulty. I am confident that I could have every firearm among the Indians of this reservation turned over to me by the individual owner inside of ten days if so ordered, each gun to be labeled with the owner's name, and a Memorandum Receipt given to him for the same, with the understanding that if not returned to him, within a certain time the respective owners would be entitled to receive compensation, at a fair valuation, for the arms thus turned in, in fact these Indians expect their guns will be required of them, and as there is no more game in this section of country, the arms being therefore useless for hunting purposes, they would willingly give them up if all were to be treated alike. An Indian with a good rifle in his hands is a very different person to the Indian without the rifle, the former is more arrogant and independent than the latter, furthermore being the possessor of a rifle he makes long journeys in quest of game, also to gratify his longings for the chase and old Indian life, which with the scarcity of game brings him small returns. Such journeys by armed Indians alarm settlers in the section of country through which they pass. I would not, however, recommend the disarming of friendly Indians, while the more turbulent and aggressive were permitted to retain their arms, and with the disarming of Indians should come Congressional legislation that would prohibit the sale of arms and ammunition, or the loan of same, to Indians, in order to render the disarming of any effect; the enactment of such a law, cannot in my opinion, be too strongly recommended to contain such penalty clauses as will keep arms from the possession of Indians in any case whatever, this for the peace and welfare of the Sioux people.

As to there being any Indians of the reservation whose character and general demeanor is such as to require, for the peace and welfare of the Indians of the surrounding communities and for the public service, that they may be removed from the reservation, I would state that there are two Indians now here "Circling Hawk" and "Iron White Man," who *were* fit subjects for discipline last summer and their names were submitted for such discipline in my telegram of November 21, last, but since the death of "Sitting Bull" their whole demeanor has changed and they are now thoroughly subdued.

An Indian named "Strike the Kettle," who is now one of the prisoners at Fort Sully, was one of the two Indians who fired the first two shots into the Indian police at the time Sitting Bull was arrested on December 15th, last. He was wounded in the leg but managed to escape and fled with the others towards the Cheyenne River Reservation. The chastisement inflicted upon these parties by the police in the Grand River affair and the subsequent suffering they experienced in reaching Cheyenne River Agency with eight of their number who joined Big Foot, killed in the Wounded Knee affair, I believe their punishment to have been ample and the effect salutory, and I do not believe it to be necessary from present indications, to inflict further punishment upon individuals unless they should commit themselves in some other manner which I hardly look for from them in future.

In conclusion I would add that everything possible should be done to bring about a gradual reduction, until entirely discontinued, of the pauperizing free ration that is now issued to the Sioux Indians.

I am, Sir,

Very respectfully,

Your obd't. serv't.,

James McLaughlin,

U. S. Indian Agent.

Standing Rock Agency, May 19, 1891.

Hon. T. J. Morgan,

Commissioner of Indian Affairs, Washington, D. C.

Sir:

I have the honor to acknowledge the receipt of your communication of May 12, 1891, Land 14757-1891, 16413-1891, transmitting copy of a letter from Captain Chas. G. Penney, Acting Agent at Pine Ridge Agency, in which he reports that frequent source of evil amongst the Indians there is the constant arrival upon the reservation of Indians from other reservations—notably from Rosebud, Cheyenne River and Standing Rock Agencies—who roam over the Pine Ridge Reservation and talk trouble, etc., etc.

Captain Penney's letter is something like Shakespeare's play "Much Ado About Nothing," as far as Standing Rock Agency is concerned and in his manifest misrepresentations of facts in that respect scarcely conceals the ultimate object in view of the Military to obtain entire control of the Indians.

There are no Indians absent from this reservation nor have any absented themselves during the past winter other than those who fled to Cheyenne River and Pine Ridge Agencies last December and have not yet returned, and with one single individual exception I distinctly deny Captain Penney's statement to the effect that Indians from this reservation are constantly arriving at Pine Ridge Agency.

The case referred to was the case of a young Indian named Charles Whitebull, who speaks and understands English and is otherwise very intelligent. This young man was then and is now an enlisted Military Indian Scout, who was given a furlough by the Commanding Officer of Fort Yates for the purpose of visiting his wife's people at Pine Ridge, who had fled from here on December 15, last. The principal object of the Post Commander in granting the furlough was, however, to gain information from the Indians at Pine Ridge with regard to future prospects of hostilities and the general feeling amongst them in regard to the late troubles and the effect of the Sitting Bull and Wounded Knee affairs upon their future conduct, and Charles Whitebull was instructed I believe to make such inquiries secretly with a view to obtaining such information and reporting the same to the Commanding Officer of Fort Yates upon his return, and Whitebull fulfilled his mission faithfully.

I would further state that I have not issued a single pass to Pine Ridge or Rosebud Agencies since early last October, and any Indians absent without a pass would be promptly reported to me by our vigilant Indian police, and no such reports have been made.

There are always persons to be found at an Indian
Agency who are ready to manifest a great desire to furnish information to the "powers that be," especially to a
new Agent, and are ever ready to report any little rumor
they may hear or reason out, taking care that it will be
that which they think will be pleasing to the ear they wish
it to reach, and I regard much of the sensational reports
coming from Pine Ridge Agency of that nature.

I am, Sir,

Very respectfully,

Your obed't. serv't.,

    James McLaughlin,

    U. S. Indian Agent.

APPENDIX NO. 3

REPORT OF THE COMMISSIONER OF
INDIAN AFFAIRS—1891—Vol. I.

Report of James McLaughlin, U. S. Indian Agent, Fort Yates, North Dakota, Page 328 beginning at 7th paragraph and continuing to 11th line of 2nd paragraph on page 329; page 333 to 4th paragraph page 334, and last paragraph of same page; page 335, beginning at 2nd paragraph and continuing to 2nd paragraph of page 336; page 337, 4th, 5th, 10th and 11th paragraphs; page 338.

On October 17, 1890, I wrote the following letter:

Standing Rock Agency, October 17, 1890.

Hon. T. J. Morgan,

    Commissioner of Indian Affairs.

Sir:

    Referring to the subject of office letter "L" dated June 7, last, and my reply of the 18th of same month relative to rumors of a prospective outbreak among the Sioux, I have the honor to state that there is now considerable excitement and some disaffection existing among certain Indians of this agency.

    I trust that I may not be considered an alarmist and believe that my past record among the Sioux will remove any doubt in this respect, and I do not wish to be understood as considering the present state of excitement so alarming as to apprehend any immediate uprising or serious outcome, but I do feel it my duty to report the present "craze" and nature of the excitement existing among the Sitting Bull faction of Indians over the expected Indian millennium, the annihilation of the white men and supremacy of the Indian, which is looked for in the near future and promised by the Indian medicine men as not later than next spring, when the new grass begins to appear, and is known among the Sioux as the return of the ghosts.

They are promised by some members of the Sioux tribe, who have lately developed into medicine men, that the Great Spirit has promised them that their punishment by the dominant race has been sufficient and that their numbers having now become so decimated, will be reinforced by all Indians who are dead; that the dead are all returning to reinhabit this earth which belongs to the Indians; that they are driving back with them as they return immense herds of buffalo and elegant wild horses to have for the catching; that the Great Spirit promises them that the white man will be unable to make gunpowder in future, and all attempts at such will be a failure, and that the gunpowder now on hand will be useless as against Indians, as it will not throw a bullet with sufficient force to pass through the skin of an Indian; that the Great Spirit had deserted the Indians for a long period, but is now with them and against the whites, and will cover the earth over with 30 feet of additional soil, well sodded and timbered, under which the whites will all be smothered, and any whites who may escape this great phenomena will become small fishes in the rivers of the country; but in order to bring about this happy result the Indians must do their part and become believers and thoroughly organize.

It would seem impossible that any person, no matter how ignorant, could be brought to believe such absurd nonsense, but as a matter of fact a great many of the Indians of this agency actually believe it, and since this new doctrine has been engrafted here from the more southern

Sioux agencies, the infection has been wonderful, and so pernicious that it now includes some of the Indians who were formerly numbered with the progressive and more intelligent, and many of our very best Indians appear dazed and undecided when talking of it, their inherent superstition having been thoroughly aroused.

Sitting Bull is high priest and leading apostle of this latest Indian absurdity; in a word he is the chief mischief-maker at this agency, and if he were not here this craze, so general among the Sioux, would never have gotten a foothold at this agency. Sitting Bull is a man of low cunning, devoid of a single manly principle in his nature or an honorable trait of character, but on the contrary is capable of instigating and inciting others (those who believe in his powers) to do any amount of mischief. He is a coward and lacks moral courage; he will never lead where there is danger, but is an adept in influencing his ignorant henchmen and followers, and there is no knowing what he may direct them to attempt.

(*Signed*) James McLaughlin.

Colonel Cody (Buffalo Bill) with 8 civilian companions left the agency at 11:00 A. M. on November 29 for Sitting Bull's camp, which was 40 miles distant, and four hours after his departure a dispatch was received by the post commander of Fort Yates from Army headquarters directing the suspension of the arrest of Sitting Bull and other Indians, and couriers were at once sent after the party to notify them of the fact. Cody and party returned to the post the following morning and immediately left for the East, and the following telegram was received by me the following day:

Washington, December 1, 1890.

To James McLaughlin, Agent:

By direction of the Secretary during the present Indian troubles you are instructed that while you shall continue all the business and carry into effect the educational and other purposes of your agency you will as to

all operations intended to suppress any outbreak by force
cooperate with and obey the orders of the military officers commanding on the reservation in your charge.

R. V. Belt,
Acting Commissioner.

From the active movements of the military I foresaw that the
arrest of Sitting Bull was liable to be ordered at any moment and
such order might come at an inopportune time, so to avoid trouble
I contemplated making the arrest on Saturday night, December 6,
when everything was most favorable, for it, and on December 5,
sent the following dispatch. Other dispatches on the subject are
also given:

Standing Rock Agency, December 5, 1890.
To Commissioner Indian Affairs:

Everything quiet at present; weather cold and snowing. Am I authorized to arrest Sitting Bull and other
fomentors of mischief when I think best?

McLaughlin,
Agent.

Washington, December 5, 1890.
To McLaughlin, Agent:

Replying to your telegram of this date Secretary
directs that you make no arrests whatever except under
orders of the military or upon an order from the Secretary of the Interior.

R. V. Belt,
Acting Commissioner.

St. Paul, Minn., December 6, 1890.
U. S. Indian Agent, James McLaughlin:

Referring to telegram sent Colonel Drum, which he
will show you, is there any change of condition recently

which makes present action specially necessary? As you know I am disposed to support you. Some prior movements I would like to see completed.

Ruger,
Brigadier-General, Commanding.

Standing Rock Agency, December 6, 1890.
To Gen. Ruger,
St. Paul, Minn.

No change in condition except for the better. Sitting Bull can be kept on reserve by Indian police without fear of escape before arrest is required, which can be made by Indian police, but in my judgment there is no necessity for immediate arrest. Postponement preferable, as every day of cold weather cools the ardor of the dancers. This is beef-ration day and everything is quiet.

McLaughlin,
Agent.

HEAQUARTERS DEPARTMENT OF DAKOTA
St. Paul, Minn., December 12, 1890.
To Commanding Officer,
Ft. Yates, N. Dak.:

The division commander has directed that you make it your especial duty to secure the person of Sitting Bull. Call on Indian agent to cooperate and render such assistance as will best promote the purpose in view. Acknowledge receipt and, if not perfectly clear, repeat back.

By command of General Ruger.

M. Barber,
Asst. Adj.-General.

(Copy furnished by commanding officer, Fort Yates.)

The following report of the occurrences following the date of General Ruger's dispatch, made by me to the Indian Office December

24, 1890, will show what action was taken upon the receipt of that telegram, and its results.

Seeing in the public press of the country so many absurd reports and ridiculous accounts regarding the arrest and death of "Sitting Bull," I feel called upon in justice to the Indians of this agency, 80 per cent of whom are loyal and well disposed, and in justice to the police force in particular, to give the following statement of facts which I desire given to the Associated Press or some of the leading journals of the country. By way of preface I desire to say that "Sitting Bull," who was constitutionally a bad man without a redeeming quality, has been growing worse during the past year, so that his aggressiveness had assumed proportions of open rebellion against constituted authority, notwithstanding that every honorable means to change him from his imprudent, course had been resorted to.

On or about the 15th of October last, while Kicking Bear, who came from Cheyenne River Reservation upon an invitation from Sitting Bull to organize a ghost dance at his camp, he (Sitting Bull) broke his pipe of peace, which he had kept in his house since his surrender as a prisoner of war in July, 1881. When asked why he had broken that pipe, he replied that he wanted to die and wanted to fight.

For some reason best known to himself, Sitting Bull had absented himself from the agency on the biweekly ration days (he had usually been present) since October 25, last, and I made a special trip to his home, 40 miles from the agency, and remained in the settlement over night, to make a last effort in trying to bring him to see the evil of his course, and was somewhat encouraged by the promises then made by him; but he failed to come to the agency, as he had partly agreed to do.

I would have arrested him at his home on Saturday, the 6th instant, as the police officers had arrangements perfected and everything appeared favorable for it at that time, but an office telegram was received the previous evening which forbade the arrest until further orders.

On Friday afternoon the 12th instant an order to secure the person of Sitting Bull was received, but as I desired the arrest to be made without bloodshed, and knew the temper of his followers in their blind religious craze the wisdom of attempting it at that time was contrary to my judgment, and in consultation with Colonel Drum, post commander of Fort Yates, it was concluded to defer the matter until Saturday, the 20th, on which dates the major portion of his supporters would be at the agency for the biweekly issue of rations. In the meantime I had him kept under close surveillance by Indian Police specially detailed for that purpose.

* * *

When the final order for Sitting Bull's arrest was received on the afternoon of the 12th instant I sent a courier for Shave Head and communicated to him and directed that he take such of the other policemen as he deemed proper and report to Bull Head at Grand River as early as practicable, but not to attempt to make the arrest until further ordered, unless it was discovered that Sitting Bull was preparing to leave the reservation, which must be prevented if possible.

The policemen on duty in the Grand River settlements were engaged in procuring logs and forwarding them by teams to a point where the road crosses Oak Creek, about half way between the agency and the principle settlements on Grand River, where a shelter station (house and stable) was being erected for accommodation of persons passing over the road during the winter months, and on Saturday, the 13th, Sergeant John Eagleman left the agency with a detachment of eight police for the Oak Creek station to commence erecting the buildings referred to, also to be within supporting distance of the force operating on Grand River, if necessary. It was Men the intention of the police not to make the arrest until Saturday morning, the 20th instant as above stated, which was believed to be the most practical way to obviate excitement and trouble, as at that date most of the Indians would be in at the agency for rations; but on Sunday, the 14th instant, at 4 P. M., Special Policeman Hawkman No. 1 arrived at the agency from Grand River with a letter to me from Lieutenant Bull Head, written by Mr. John M. Carignan, teacher of the Grand River School, dated at Grand River, December 14, 12:30 A. M., containing the information that Sitting Bull was preparing to leave the reservation, and that they (the police) wanted to arrest him without further delay, giving as their reason that he (Sitting Bull) had been fitting his horses for a long and hard ride and that, being well mounted, if he once got the start of them they would be unable to overtake him.

I had just finished the letter referred to, and commenced questioning the courier as to the disposition Lieut. Bull Head had made of the additional force of police sent him, when Colonel Drum, the post commander, came into my office and I showed him the letter. Colonel Drum remarked that, under his orders received the previous Friday, the arrest must be made without further delay, and upon further consultation we concluded that it should be made the following morning, and for the salutary effect that it would have upon the Indians I desired to have the arrest made by the agency police with the troops to make a night march to Oak Creek, so as to be within supporting distance of the police, if needed, and to aid in bringing Sitting Bull safely to the agency, if pursued by his followers; also to let the Indians understand that the troops were ready to cooperate with the Indian police and assist in putting down any lawlessness among them when necessary; but above everything else I desired to have the arrest made without bloodshed, which I believed the police would be able to effect.

Before Colonel Drum left my office I wrote two letters, one in English and a translation of it into the Sioux language, both of which I sent to Lieutenant Bull Head by Second Sergeant Red Tomahawk, a very cool and reliable policeman, with orders to make the arrest. I made known to Sergeant Red Tomahawk the plan of arrest and also gave him verbal orders to take Sergeant Eagleman and his detachment from Oak Creek along with him and report to Bull Head with all possible dispatch. I had previously impressed upon the Lieutenant and First Sergeant the importance of having a light wagon with them when they went to make the arrest so that they could put Sitting Bull into it as soon as they had made him prisoner and to drive out of the Village as rapidly as possible before his followers (crazed ghost dancers) had time to assemble, which would consume but little time; whereas if too much time were wasted, it would give them an opportunity to assemble round the house and a disturbance might be created. But upon receipt of permission to make the arrest the enthusiasm among the police was so great that they neglected to take the wagon along, but went on horse back and rode boldly through the camp and up to Sitting Bull's house, where they dismounted just as daybreak began to appear.

Sitting Bull had two log cabins a few rods distant from each other, the wagon road passing between, and 10 policemen entered one of the houses and eight entered the other, so as to make sure of finding him. They found him in the larger building of the two and announced the object of their mission, which was that he was their prisoner and was to accompany them to the agency (the police also took possession of 2 rifles and 4 hunting knives, found in the house). Sitting Bull said: "Alright; I will go with you; I will put on my clothes," and then sent one of his wives to the other house for some clothing that he desired to wear; he also requested that his favorite horse be brought from the stable and saddled for him to ride, which was done by one of the policemen. While dressing, Sitting Bull caused considerable delay, and commenced abusing the policemen for disturbing him; all of which abuse they bore patiently. During this time his followers began to congregate, and when he was dressed and brought out of the house the followers had the police entirely surrounded and pressed in close to the building. Sitting Bull then became very much excited and positively refused to go with the police, and called upon his followers to rescue him. The police force, in the meantime, were reasoning with the crowd to let them pass out unmolested and at the same time gradually forced the Indians back so as to get Sitting Bull away in safety.

Lieutenant Bull Head and Sergeant Shave Head stood one on each side of Sitting Bull, with Second Sergeant Red Tomahawk behind him, to prevent his escape. At this juncture, with the excitement at its height, Catch the Bear and Strike the Kettle, two of

Sitting Bull's main supporters, dashed through the crowd, and Catch the Bear fired and the ball struck Lieutenant Bull Head on the right side. Bull Head then fired at Sitting Bull, the ball striking him on the left side between the tenth and eleventh ribs (there was no exit). Sitting Bull also received a gunshot wound in the right cheek just below the eye, and Sergeant Shave Head was at the same moment shot by Strike the Kettle, and all three fell together. Catch the Bear, who shot the Lieutenant was immediately shot and killed by Private of Police "Alone Man," and the fight then became general, in fact, a hand to hand conflict, 39 policemen and 4 volunteers against 150 Indians. The police soon drove the Indians from around the building, then charged and drove them into the woods, about 20 rods distant; after which the police returned to the building and carried their dead and wounded into Sitting Bull's house and held the buildings without further casualties, from about 5:30 A. M., to 8:30 A. M., when the cavalry command of 100 men under Captain E. G. Fechet, Eighth United States Cavalry, came in sight when the ghost dancers who were hid in the adjoining woods fled up Grand River, but after going up a short distance turned south across the prairie and through to the Moreau River and Cherry Creek, on the Cheyenne River Reservation.

The following are extracts from the report of Captain E. G. Fechet, Eighth Cavalry, commanding the detachment of cavalry, to his superiors with regard to this affair:

I can not too strongly commend the splendid courage and ability which characterized the conduct of the Indian Police commanded by Bull Head and Shave Head throughout the encounter. The attempt to arrest Sitting Bull was so managed as to place the responsibility for the fight that ensued upon Sitting Bull's band, which began the firing. Red Tomahawk assumed command of the police force after both Bull Head and Shave Head had been wounded, and it was he also, who, under circumstances requiring personal courage to the highest degree, assisted Hawkman to escape with a message to the troops. After the fight no demoralization seemed to exist among them, and they were ready and willing to cooperate with the troops to any extent desired.

* * *

Extract from my official report to the Honorable Commissioner of Indian Affairs, dated December 16th, 1890, as to the affair on Grand River:

>The details of the battle show that the Indian police behaved nobly and exhibited the best of judgment and bravery, and a recognition by the Government for their services on this occasion is richly deserved and should be promptly given with a substantial allowance for the families of those who are dead, and also for the survivors, to show them that the Government recognizes the great service that has been done for the country in the result of yesterday's fight.
>
>I respectfully urge that the Interior Department co-operate with the War Department in obtaining Congressional action which will insure to these brave survivors, and to the families of the dead, a full and generous reward. Besides the Indian police there were four volunteers, viz., Gray Eagle, Spotted Thunder, Otter Robe and Young Eagle, who participated in the fight, rendering good service and deserving light recognition. Gray Eagle (Gabriel Wamdihotah) is one of the judges of the court of Indian offenses, and his two sisters are Sitting Bull's wives. Until about 17 months ago he was Sitting Bull's main support.

To this the office replied:

>Washington, December 30, 1890.
>To James McLaughlin,
>   U. S. Indian Agent.
>Sir:
>   Your communication of 16th is received, wherein your report in detail the arrest and subsequent death of

Sitting Bull; speak of the bravery and good judgment of your Indian police; recommend that the noble services of the survivors receive substantial recognition; that the families of those who were killed be amply provided for, and that this department and the War Department join in an effort to obtain Congressional action to that end if necessary.

In reply, you are informed that this office will do all in its power to have Congress recognize and reward the praiseworthy and valuable service rendered by these men and to provide for the needs of the family of those who were killed, and, in the meantime, you will see to it that they do not suffer for the lack of any supplies or other requisites for their sustenance and comfort; and any specific recommendation you make in regard to them pending legislation in their favor will be carefully considered and promptly approved by me if practicable and proper.

I also desire you to publicly commend, in my name the bravery and fidelity of the force and inform the survivors that, while I sincerely regret that the taking of any life was necessary, it is very gratifying to me to know that I have such reliable assistants in my efforts to promote the welfare of their people, and that their noble conduct has been highly praised wherever spoken of.

Respectfully,

T. J. Morgan,
Commissioner.

On March 3, 1891, I suggested to the Honorable Commissioner that a pension of at least $15.00 per month be given to each of the families of Bull Head, Shave Head, and Little Eagle, and $10.00 per month to each of the families of Paul Akicitah, Hawkman No. 1, and John Armstrong, who were killed, and also $10.00 per month to Alexander Middle, who was severely wounded and will probably lose his foot. Also that each of the 33 policemen and four volunteers, survivors of the engagement, receive a medal commemorative of their fidelity, and payment at the rate of $50.00 per head for the ponies they had killed and those that stampeded during the fight.

No information has been received that this suggestion has been acted upon or that anything has been accomplished for the relief of the parties named; and I would respectfully recommend that the matter be placed before Congress early in the approaching session.

In conclusion, I venture to say that had the suggestion contained in my letter of November 19th, and afterwards repeatedly referred to in my correspondence, been adopted as to the separation of these Indians and the suspension of rations to the evil-disposed portion of them, that the dancing would have been broken up and Sitting Bull arrested without bloodshed.

No uneasiness or disaffection now exists among the Indians of this agency. All appear anxious to forget the late unpleasantness and progression is manifest among all classes.

I am, sir, very respectfully, your obedient servant.

James McLaughlin,
U. S. Indian Agent.

CASUALTIES IN THE AFFAIR ON GRAND RIVER
December 15, 1890.

1. Henry Bull Head, first lieutenant; died eighty-two hours after the fight.
2. Charles Shave Head, first sergeant; died twenty-five hours after the fight.
3. James Little Eagle, fourth sergeant; killed.
4. Paul Akicitah, private; killed.
5. John Armstrong; special; killed.
6. David Hawkman; special; killed.
7. Alexander Middle; private; wounded, will lose his foot.

1. Sitting Bull; fifty-six years old; killed.
2. Crow Foot (Sitting Bull's son), seventeen years old; killed.
3. Blackbird, forty-three years old; killed.
4. Catch the Bear, forty-four years old; killed.
5. Spotted Horn Bull, fifty-six years old; killed.

6. Brave Thunder, forty-six years old; killed.

7. Little Assinaboine, forty-four years old; killed.

8. Chase Wounded, twenty-four years old; killed.

9. Bull Ghost; wounded; entirely recovered.

10. Brave Thunder; wounded; recovering.

11. Strike the Kettle; wounded; recovered.

* * *

Major James McLaughlin's book, "My Friend the Indian," states that Sitting Bull was shot in the cheek by Red Tomahawk and that this shot killed him instantly. This statement has been authenticated by a personal interview with Major McLaughlin.

A careful search has been made of the records of the Indian and Pension Bureaus, Senate Committee on Pensions and Library of Congress, and while bills appear to have been introduced in the 52nd Congress there is no indication that any of them were ever passed. The widow of Bull Head was finally granted a pension on showing that her husband had at one time served thirty days with the military forces of the United States. Both Alexander Middle and Red Tomahawk made application for pension under the act of March 4, 1917, and both claims were rejected.

APPENDIX NO. 4

There follows in this Appendix a complete and official report of the operations of the military regarding the Grand River Engagement.

The first document is a letter of transmittal written by John W. Noble, Secretary of the Interior to Major McLaughlin.

DEPARTMENT OF THE INTERIOR

Washington, January 16, 1891.

James McLaughlin, Esq.,

U. S. Indian Agent, Standing Rock Agency, N. D.

Sir:

I enclose herewith a copy of the report of Capt. E. G. Fechet, commanding 8th Cavalry, at Fort Yates, N. D., together with report Lieut. Col. W. F. Drum, commanding the Post, to the Adjutant General, Department of Dakota, in relation to the arrest and death of Sitting Bull on the 15th ultimo.

In these reports as well as in the endorsement of the General of the Army forwarding them to the Secretary of War, special mention is made of your action as commendable and of that of the Indian Police as marked by bravery and fidelity in this affair, to which your attention is particularly invited.

Very respectfully,
　　John W. Noble,
　　Secretary.
279, Ind. Div. '91.
One enclosure.

　　　　Fort Yates, North Dakota, December 17, 1890.
To the Post Adjutant,
　　Fort Yates, N. D.
Sir:

For the information of the Commanding Officer, I have the honor to report the operations of the Battalion of the 8th Cavalry under my command for the purpose indicated in Orders No. 247 of this post, (copy attached marked "A".)

The command consisted of Troop "F," 8th Cavalry, Lieutenants Slocum and Steele and 48 enlisted men; Troop "G," 8th Cavalry, Captain Fechet, Lieutenants E. H. Crowder and E. C. Brooks, and 51 enlisted men; Captain A. R. Chapin, Medical Officer, and Acting Hospital Steward August Nickel; two Indian Scouts, Smell the Bear and Iron Dog; Mr. Louis Prinnan, Indian Department Standing Rock Agency, Guide and Interpreter.

One Gatling Gun was attached to "G" Troop and one breech-loading steel Hotchkiss gun attached to Troop "F." There was furnished the command one four-horse spring wagon carrying one day's cooked rations and one day's grain for the whole command, and one Red Cross Ambulance.

COMMANDING OFFICERS
Captain E. G. Fechet, Commanding Battalion.
Lieut. E. H. Crowder, Commanding "G" Troop.
Lieut. S. L H. Slocum, Commanding "F" Troop.
Lieut. E. C. Brooks, Commanding Field Artillery.

The command moved out at midnight, December the 14th, and by rapid marching was by daylight within three miles of Sitting Bull's camp, which is fully from 41 to 42 miles from Fort Yates.

After daybreak I expected every minute to meet the Indian Police with Sitting Bull their prisoner, it having been arranged by Major McLaughlin, Indian Agent, that they should make a descent upon Bull's camp about daybreak, arresting Bull and delivering him to me for conduct to this post. It will be seen by reference to the first paragraph of the order that the command was to proceed only to the crossing of Oak Creek, which was 18 miles from Bull's camp. After receiving this order on consultation with Colonel Drum, Commanding the post, it was decided that I should move as close to Bull's camp as possible without discovery and there await the police. A short time after dawn a mounted man was discovered approaching rapidly. This proved to be one of the police who reported that all the other police had been killed. The substance of his report with the additional statement that I would move in rapidly and endeavor to relieve any of the police who might be alive, I forwarded to the Commanding Officer.

The command was at once put into condition for immediate action. A light but extended line was thrown in advance, the main body disposed in two columns in column of fours about three hundred yards apart, the artillery between the heads of columns. A few minutes after making these dispositions another of the police came in and reported that Bull's people had a number of the police penned up in his house, that they were nearly out of ammunition and could not hold out much longer.

The command was moved with all speed to a point on the high lands overlooking the valley of Grand River and immediately opposite Sitting Bull's house and the camp of the Ghost Dancers, distant some 1500 yards.

A hasty examination showed a party of Indians, apparently 40 or 50, on a high point on our right front some

900 yards distant, but whether a party of police or friends of Bull's people could not be determined. While trying to make out the position and identity of the two parties, there were a few shots fired by the party on the hill and replied to from Sitting Bull's house; there was also firing from the woods beyond Bull's house, but on whom directed it was impossible to tell.

I caused a white flag to be erected on the crest where I was located (a pre-arranged signal between the soldiers and police) and directed a few shots to be fired from the Hotchkiss into the woods mentioned. In answer a white flag was displayed from Bull's house and Indians were seen leaving the woods going in the direction of the hills to the south across Grand River. The Hotchkiss gun was then turned upon the party on our right front; this with some fire from a dismounted line of "F" Troop caused them to retreat rapidly from their position up the valley of Grand River to the northwest.

Lieutenant Slocum with his troop dismounted was ordered to advance immediately upon the house.

Lieutenant Crowder with "G" Troop mounted moved rapidly to the right along the high lands covering the right flank of the dismounted line. As the dismounted line approached the house the police came out and joined the command.

The line was advanced through the timber dislodging a few hostiles who disappeared rapidly up the river through the willows. This line after advancing through the willows some six hundred yards, fell back to the immediate vicinity of Sitting Bull's house, leaving pickets at the furthest point gained by the advance.

Lieutenant Crowder in the meantime observed the Indians gathering at the houses up the river about two miles from Bull's camp moved in pursuit of them. The Indians fell back from every point upon the approach of the troops, not showing any desire to engage in hostile action against the soldiers.

All the houses for a distance of about two miles were examined and all were found deserted, but showed signs of recent occupation. Failing to come up with the Indians in this direction "G" Troop fell back and joined the main command at Sitting Bull's lodge. Upon arriving at this place, I found evidences of a most desperate encounter between the Agency police and Sitting Bull's followers.

In the vicinity of the house, within a radius of about 50 yards, there were found the dead bodies of eight hostiles including Sitting Bull; two horses were also killed. Within the house there were found four dead and three wounded policemen.

It was learned through the Interpreter that the hostile Indians had carried away with them one of their dead and 5 or 6 of their wounded, making an approximate total of 15 casualties in Sitting Bull's band.

A list of casualties by name on both sides is hereto attached marked "B."

From the best evidence obtainable I am led to believe that the police under command of Bull Head and Shave Head, about 40 strong, entered Sitting Bull's camp about 5:30 A. M., on the 15th instant for the purpose of making the arrest of Sitting Bull. Sitting Bull was taken from his house and while the police were parleying with him endeavoring to induce him to submit peaceably Bull Head was shot by Catch the Bear in the leg. Bull Head immediately shot and killed Sitting Bull, when the melee became general with the result heretofore given. The fight lasted but a few moments when the police secured the house and stable adjoining, driving Sitting Bull's men from the village to cover in the adjoining woods and hills. From these positions the fight was kept up until about 7:30 A. M., when the troops came up.

I learned that soon after the occupation of the house and stable by the police, volunteers were called for to carry a report of the situation back to the approaching troops. Hawk Man offered to perform this perilous service and at the imminent risk of his life, assisted by Red Tomahawk, he effected his escape being shot through his coat and gloves while engaged in the attempt. This was the first Scout met by the command.

My orders were explicit as to the arrest of Sitting Bull, but contemplated no pursuit of his band. I therefore did not feel authorized to follow the Indians up the valley, especially as I felt satisfied from the report of Lieutenant Crowder that it would only result in unnecessarily frightening peaceful Indians away from their homes, and that the withdrawal of the troops together with the messages I communicated to the Indians to the effect that the capture of Sitting Bull only was desired would tend to assure those who were loyally disposed towards their Agent.

Accordingly I gave orders for the command to withdraw to Oak Creek, of which the Commanding Officer of Fort Yates was informed by courier, with the request that he communicate his further orders to me at that point. Previous to leaving, word was sent up and down the valley to the friendly Indians of this movement in order that they might avail themselves of the protection of the troops in their withdrawal to the Agency, which they did in considerable numbers. All the dead Indian police, together with their wounded and the body of Sitting Bull were brought in by me.

Upon reaching Oak Creek at 6 P. M., I was met by a courier who informed me that the Commanding Officer of Fort Yates with two companies of Infantry and ten days supplies would reach Oak Creek some time in the night. Upon their arrival at 12 o'clock I turned over the command.

I cannot too strongly commend the splendid courage and ability which characterized the conduct of the Indian Police commanded by Bull Head and Shave Head throughout the encounter. The attempt to arrest Sitting Bull was so managed as to place the responsibility for the fight that ensued, upon Sitting Bull's band, which began the firing.

Red Tomahawk assumed the command of the police after both Bull Head and Shave Head had been wounded, and it was he who under circumstances requiring personal courage to the highest degree, assisted Hawk Man to effect his escaped with a message to the troops. After the fight no demoralization seemed to exist among the police and they were ready and willing to cooperate with the troops to any extent desired.

The attention of the Commanding Officer is invited to the celerity of this movement. In brief the command marched from here to Sitting Bull's camp and back to Oak Creek in 17 hours. This with the ground covered in getting into position and the demonstration to the right by Lieutenant Crowder, made a total distance of at least 70 miles. It must be taken into consideration that the movement back to Oak Creek, 18 miles, was made very slowly.

Thus it will be seen that the march out, including the movements into position were made at the rate of over 6 miles an hour.

During the whole march the column moved steadily without stretching out or closing up, a most satisfactory commentary upon the drill and discipline of the two troops composing my command.

To say less would be a want of appreciation on my part of the command under my orders.

(*Signed*) E. G. Fechet,
Captain Eighth Cavalry, Commanding.
    Official copy:
    W. F. Drum,
    Lieutenant Colonel Twelfth Infantry.

Fort Yates, N. D., December 14, 1890.

ORDERS,
No. 247.

EXTRACT

II.—Captain E. G. Fechet, 8th Cavalry, will proceed with Troops "F" and "G," 8th Cavalry, the Hotchkiss gun and one Gatling gun to the crossing of Oak Creek by the Sitting Bull Road, for the purpose of preventing the escape or rescue of Sitting Bull should the Indian police succeed in arresting him.

The command will move out at 12 o'clock midnight in light marching order, and will be supplied with 50 rounds of carbine and 12 rounds of revolver ammunition per man, 4,000 rounds of ammunition for Gatling gun, one day's cooked rations and one day's forage.

After receiving the prisoner Captain Fechet will return with his command to this post, reporting to the Commanding Officer on arrival.

If one arrival at Oak Creek Captain Fechet learns that the police are fighting or need assistance, he will push on and if necessary follow Sitting Bull as long as possible with his supplies, keeping the Post Commander informed by courier of his movements.

The march will be so regulated as to reach Oak Creek by 6:30 A. M., tomorrow the 15th instant.

Should arrest be made every precaution will be taken to prevent escape or rescue.

Two Indian Scouts will accompany the command.

Assistant Surgeon A. R. Chapin, Medical Department, will report to Captain Fechet for duty with the expedition.

First Lieutenant S. L. H. Slocum, 8th Cavalry, with Troop "F," will report to Captain Fechet for orders.

Second Lieutenant E. C. Brooks, 8th Cavalry, will also report to Captain Fechet for duty with the expedition.

One Hospital ambulance with necessary supplies will accompany the expedition, the Quartermaster furnishing the necessary team.

By order of Lieutenant Colonel W. F. Drum.

(*Signed*) E. C. Brooks,

Second Lieutenant, Eighth Cavalry, Post Adjutant.
Official copy:
(*Signed*) W. F. Drum,
Lieutenant Colonel Twelfth Infantry.

CASUALTIES IN THE POLICE FORCE

Henry Tatankapah (Bull Head), First Lieutenant in command. Dangerously wounded, 4 wounds, since dead.

Charles Kashdah (Shave Head), First Sergeant. Mortally wounded, since dead.

James Wambdchigalah (Little Eagle), Fourth Sergeant. Killed.

Alexander Hochokah (Middle) Private. Painfully wounded.

Paul Akichitah (Afraid of Soldiers), Private. Killed.

John Armstrong, Special Police. Killed.

Hawk Man No. 2, Special Police. Killed.

CASUALTIES IN THE HOSTILES

1. Sitting Bull.
2. Black Bird.
3. Catch the Bear.
4. Little Assinaboine.
5. Crow Foot (Sitting Bull's son).
6. Spotted Horn Bull (a chief).
7. Brave Thunder (a chief)
8. Chase Wounded
   Official copy:
   W. F. Drum,
   Lieutenant Colonel, Twelfth Infantry.

12:30 A. M.,
Grand River, December 14, 1890.

Major James McLaughlin,
   Standing Rock Agency, N. D. Dear
Sir:

"Bull Head" wishes to report what occurred at Sitting Bull's camp at a Council held yesterday.

It seems that Sitting Bull has received a letter from the Pine Ridge outfit, asking him to come over there as God was to appear to them.

Sitting Bull's people want him to go, but he has sent a letter to you asking your permission, and if you do not give it, he is going to go anyway, he has been fitting up his horses, to stand a long ride and will go a horseback in case he is pursued.

Bull Head would like to arrest him at once before he has the chance of giving them the slip, as he thinks that if he gets the start, it will be impossible to catch him, if you should want to arrest him, he says to send word to him by courier immediately, also to let him know what your plans are, if soldiers are to come, he says to send them by Sitting Bull's road.

He also mentions something about "Shave Head" coming down here, but as I am not good enough interpreter to understand everything he has said you can use your own judgment in regards to that, one thing I understand thoroughly, and that is, that the poor man is eaten out of house and home, he says that what with councils and couriers coming to his place, that even the hay he had is very nearly all gone, I sympathize with him, as I am nearly in the same boat.

If you send a dispatch to Bull Head through me, please send me some envelopes as I am entirely out, can't even find one to enclose this letter.

Yours very respectfully,

(*Signed*) John M. Carignan.

A true copy,

G. H. Patten,

Second Lieutenant, Twenty-Second Infantry, Acting Post Adjutant.

Fort Yates, N. D., December 17th, 1890.

The Assistant Adjutant General,

Department of Dakota, Saint Paul, Minn.

Sir:

I have the honor to report that on Sunday, the 14th instant, Agent McLaughlin received a letter from John M. Carignan, school teacher on Grand River, (copy enclosed marked A), indicating that Sitting Bull was preparing to leave the Reservation, and that Bull Head, the Lieutenant of Police, was anxious to attempt his arrest. It was found on inquiry that there was not more than twenty lodges in the immediate vicinity of Sitting Bull's house. In accordance with telegraphic instructions of December 12, 1890, and after consultation with Agent McLaughlin, it was determined to order the arrest of Sitting Bull by the Indian Police, about forty of whom had already been assembled in that vicinity as a precautionary measure. The arrest was to be attempted before daylight on Monday, the 15th instant, Bull Head in charge, and with strict instructions that Sitting Bull must not escape or be rescued.

I then ordered Troops F and G, 8th Cavalry, with one Gatling and one Hotchkiss gun—Captain E. G. Fechet, 8th Cavalry Commanding—to move out Sunday night, in light marching order, to meet the Police on their way in with Sitting Bull, to prevent rescue on the road—the Cavalry not to start before midnight so that an Indian runner could not give the alarm before the Indian Police had acted.

At about 12:30 P. M., 15th instant, I received word from Captain Fechet that at 7:30 A. M. he was within three miles of Sitting Bull's camp and was met by a policeman who informed him that the police and Indians were fighting; that Sitting Bull had been arrested and afterwards killed to prevent his escape. That the Cavalry would push on as rapidly as possible to the assistance of the police.

On receipt of this information, and not knowing how large a force the hostiles might have, nor how long it might be necessary for the Cavalry to remain out, they having no baggage nor rations, I moved out of the post for Grand River at 2:30 P. M. with 30 men of Company H and 37 of Company G, 12th Infantry, (as many men as I thought it safe to take from the post) 10 days rations, 10 days forage, and necessary camp equipage for both Cavalry and Infantry. To do this I was obliged to hire six two horse wagons to haul forage.

On the march I received more assuring dispatches from Captain Fechet, but thought it best to push on. Owing to the heavily loaded wagons I did not reach Oak Creek until 11:30 P. M. Distance 22 miles.

I found the Cavalry at Oak Creek, to which point Captain Fechet had returned. Went into camp and at 10 o'clock A. M., next day, finding that the hostiles had scattered, and that if I moved forward to Grand River I would probably do more harm than good, I broke camp and returned with the whole force to this post.

Enclosed is Captain Fechet's report of the operations of the Cavalry, marked "B." The energy displayed by Captain Fechet and the officers and men of his command in getting to the assistance of the police and in disbursing the hostiles is highly commendable.

The officers present with the two Companies of Infantry were: Captain Craigie and Lieutenant Uline, Company G, and Captain Haskell and Lieutenant Baker, Company H. Both officers and men showed fine spirit, and if they had had an opportunity would have done good service.

The distance marched between 2:30 P. M. on the 15th and 5 P. M. on the 16th was forty-four miles.

To do this with troops just out of barracks it was necessary to assist them by permitting a few at a time to ride on wagons.

Both Cavalry and Infantry are in good condition and ready for any future service.

Too much cannot be said of the excellent conduct of the police. Had they been better armed and been well supplied with ammunition I am of the opinion that many more of the hostile would have fallen.

I earnestly recommend that Congress be asked to provide for the wounded Indian police and for the families of those who were killed. No soldiers could have rendered better service, and it would probably encourage other Indians.

Agent McLaughlin has rendered most valuable assistance by his advice, by furnishing information, and by his able management of the police force, which is composed of picked men.

For list of killed and wounded see paper attached to Captain Fechet's report.

Very respectfully,

Your obedient servant,

    (*Signed*) W. F. Drum,

    Lieutenant Colonel, Twelfth Infantry, Commanding Post.

    Official copy:

    W. F. Drum,

    Lieutenant Colonel, Twelfth Infantry.

1ST ENDORSEMENT

Headquarters Division of the Missouri,

    In the Field, Rapid City, S. D.,

    December 28, 1890.

Respectfully forwarded to the Adjutant General, U. S. A., with copy of my communication to General Ruger relating to this arrest.

    (*Signed*) Nelson A. Miles,

    Major General, Commanding.

Copy

TELEGRAM

HEADQUARTERS DIVISION OF THE MISSOURI

Rapid City, S. D., December 27, 1890.

General Thomas H. Ruger,

    Commanding Department of Dakota, St. Paul, Minn.

    The Division Commander has read the official report of Lieutenant Colonel Drum, 12th Infantry, and Captain Fechet, 8th Cavalry, regarding the arrest of Sitting Bull. He desires me to express his approval of the good judgment displayed by the officers, and the assistance of the Agent, the fortitude of the troops and bravery of the Indian police.

    It required no ordinary courage to go out into an Indian camp of well armed warriors and arrest the chief conspirator on the eve of his departure to join the large body of his following, then in defiant hostility to the Government, and engaged in robbing its citizens and looting their homes.

    It was from Sitting Bull that emissaries have been for months going to other tribes, inciting them to hostility, and he died while resisting the lawful officials of the Government. Even after he had been peaceably arrested, he raised the cry of a revolt and incited his men to shoot down the Government police in the lawful discharge of their duty.

    The fearless action of Captain Fechet and his command entitles them to great credit, and the celerity of his movements showed the true soldierly spirit.

    The Division Commander desires that his sympathy be expressed to those who have suffered from wounds, and the families of the dead, brave, loyal Indian police, and his thanks to all who took part in this arrest, that has already resulted in the surrender of more than one hundred defiant, lawless savages, and with other measures

THE LAST DAYS OF SITTING BULL

has done much to prevent the destruction of many peaceable homes and innocent lives.

By command of Major General Miles.

(*Signed*) Marion P. Maus,

First Lieutenant, First Infantry, Aide-de-Camp.

HEADQUARTERS OF THE ARMY

Washington, January 5, 1891.

Respectfully submitted to the Secretary of War, with the suggestion that a copy be furnished to the Department of the Interior with special reference to the commendation of the conduct of Agent McLaughlin, and the bravery of the Indian police, in which I cordially concur.

(*Signed*) J. M. Schofield,

Major General Commanding.

APPENDIX NO. 5

Major James McLaughlin first published his book entitled "My Friend The Indian" in 1910, Houghton Mifflin & Company being the publishers. A second edition was published in 1916 and a third edition in 1926. In this edition George Bird Grinnell contributed a valuable introduction.

At the death of Major McLaughlin in 1923, all his books, manuscripts and papers came into the possession of Mrs. R. S. McLaughlin, of McLaughlin, South Dakota, a daughter-in-law of the Major. In 1931 the writer examined these papers and among them discovered the manuscript of the book "My Friend the Indian." In the original manuscript there were three chapter not contained in the published book. As the manuscript was originally written, these chapters were Numbers 13, 14 and 15. Later among these papers it was found that all three chapters had been rejected by the publishers in1910, the reason not appearing for the rejection.

Chapter 13 is entitled, "Sitting Bull's Death Aftermath."

Chapter 14 is entitled, "How Hawkman Rode to His Death."

Chapter 15 is entitled, "Shave Head's Code of Honor."

For twenty-five years these missing chapters remained unpublished. They were published for the first time by the author in 1936 in a pamphlet entitled "My Friend, The Indian." No change has been made in any statements or the language in which these statements were made. Those who read them now may rely that they are the actual writings of the Major though written many years ago. There is no question but what these chapters throw additional light on the many stirring events relating to the Sioux Trouble on Grand River in 1890, and for that reason they are published as contributions to the History of the Sioux.

My Friend The Indian contains such an amazing and authentic history of that period in which the savage Sioux were brought under the influence of our civilization, that it has been widely read, necessitating three editions. The story there published is not complete without adding thereto Chapters Thirteen, Fourteen and Fifteen, which have been omitted from all editions.

MY FRIEND THE INDIAN
CHAPTER THIRTEEN
SITTING BULL'S DEATH AFTERMATH

*How He was Martyrized by the
Sensational Press and His Taking Off
Made the Subject of Official Correspondence*

The death of Sitting Bull and its circumstances made that worthy a martyr at the hands of the sensational press—which had been demanding his suppression for months—but elicited from the authorities understanding the situation instant sympathetic appreciation of the merits of the policemen who had died in doing a duty for which they should have been thanked by the whole country. The arrest of Sitting Bull was demanded—made necessary—as a peace measure. If he had been allowed to continue stirring up the Indian people, if he had not been summarily prevented from leaving the Reservation as he intended, there is no possible doubt that he would have led an outbreak that might have cost hundreds of lives and the outlay of much treasure in its suppression. His death was an incident of the arrest of a desperate man surrounded by even more desperate followers. As an act of blood-letting it was to be deplored, but it was not to be thought of in the face of the fact that several brave and determined men who had no other object than the carrying out of orders given them officially, had lost their lives through his demand that his people shoot down his captors. I regretted the death of Sitting Bull not only because the act that precipitated it brought about the killing of six Indian policemen, together with himself and seven of his staunchest supporters, and although the elimination of the old medicine man was necessary for the welfare of the community, I was exceedingly sorry over his demise at the time and the way that it occurred. I stood for peace, the peace of the community and welfare of the well-disposed Indians, and thought that the arrest would be made without bloodshed. It was not the shedding of Sitting Bull's blood that I regretted so much as I did the killing of the loyal Indian policemen who were shot down by crazed fanatics on Sitting Bull's order. And he brought on the trouble which ended in his death and also the killing of much better men than he was.

It was, therefore, with some surprise that my attention was called shortly after the bloody event of December 15, 1890, to the fact that some newspapers were inclined to find fault with the manner of the arrest and death of Sitting Bull. It was charged that he was unjustifiably killed—and the charge was made generally by the people and papers that had been clamoring all summer for the extinction of the old mischief-maker. I had paid no attention to these clamors hitherto and was not disposed to give them heed after the event. But I believe that the official correspondence and comment on the death of Sitting Bull, and the putting down by official proofs of the absurd stories that became current in the weeks immediately succeeding the bloody affair on Grand River, should be set forth here. I do not do this as a matter of self-justification; that was never necessary. The part I had in the affair was merely that of an official whose business it was to preserve the peace. I had the prompt and cordial support of my superiors and, if I sought gratification, had the satisfaction of knowing that the general commanding the Department, and the major general of the army of the United States, in their official reports commended my action in the matter.

But there still linger in the minds of some people—impressed at the time by the publication of fakes about the murder of Sitting

Bull, the theft of his body for the purpose of putting it on exhibition, and other yarns equally absurd—erroneous ideas that should be dissipated and I am minded to close this section of my career by giving some of the official correspondence and reports concerning the event. This is not by the way of apology or self-justification, but merely a rounding out of the story I have endeavored to record.

December 16, 1890, Colonel Drum reported the matter in detail to the military authorities—at whose instance the arrest was essayed—and on the same day I made a detailed report to the Indian Office. In response to my report I received the following from Commissioner of Indian Affairs, T. J. Morgan:

Washington, December 30, 1890.

James McLaughlin,

U. S. Indian Agent, Standing Rock, N. D.

Sir:

Your communication of the 16th inst. is received wherein you report in detail the arrest and subsequent death of Sitting Bull, speak of the bravery and good judgment of your Indian police, recommend that the noble services of the survivors receive substantial recognition, that the families of those who were killed will be amply provided for, and that this department and the War Department join in an effort to obtain congressional action to that end if necessary.

In reply you are informed that this office will do all in its power to have Congress recognize and reward the praiseworthy and valuable services rendered by these men and to provide for the needs of the families of those who were killed and, in the meantime, you will see to it that they do not suffer for lack of any supplies or requisites for their sustenance and comfort, and any specific recommendation you may make in regard to them, pending legislation in their favor, will be carefully considered and promptly approved by me, if practicable and proper.

I also desire you to publicly commend in my name the bravery and fidelity of the force and inform the survivors that, while I sincerely regret that the taking of life was necessary, it is gratifying to me to know that I have such reliable assistants in my efforts to promote the welfare of these people and that their noble conduct has been highly praised wherever spoken of.

Respectfully,

T. J. Morgan,

Commissioner.

This sufficiently voices the sentiments of the Indian Office of that day regarding the action of the Indian Police at Standing Rock. I state it now, as a regrettable fact, that the proposed Congressional action for the relief of the families of the men who died in the affair on Grand River is still in contemplation. Successive Congresses have failed to find time or money to provide for the families of the red heroes who laid down their lives that morning and prevented what I verily believe would have been a disastrous outbreak. So much for the claims of the red widows and orphans.

In response to a further report made by me by telegraph and evoked by the necessity for showing what was going on at the Standing Rock Reservation, while war was imminent on other Sioux Reservations, I received the following from Commissioner Morgan:

Washington, January 12, 1891.

James McLaughlin,

U. S. Indian Agent, Standing Rock, N. D.

Sir:

I have read with gratification your telegram of the 10th inst., and am glad to know that the Standing Rock Indians have been so very generally loyal to the Government.

Please say to the Indians of your agency that I very much regret the loss of life that has occurred. It has been a very sad matter to me as well as the Indians. I appreciate the fact that those who have remained steadfast and have taken no part in the hostilities have done so against the entreaties of some of their friends and sometimes at considerable cost to themselves. They will see plainly hereafter that they chose the wise course and that those who did otherwise made a miserable mistake. I rejoice at the loyalty which they have manifested in this trying time and will do everything in my power to promote their prosperity.

I also wish to express my appreciation of the skill and firmness with which you have held the Standing Rock Indians and managed the affairs of the Agency, and I trust that peace and progress among the Indians will abundantly witness to the wisdom and efficiency of your administration.

Very respectfully,

T. J. Morgan,

Commissioner.

This was written at the time when the Indians at the other agencies were in a ferment and just subsequent to the Wounded Knee disaster at Pine Ridge Agency.

At the moment, the Indians of the Standing Rock Reservation were under absolute control, yet there could be no doubt that there was a great deal of excitement among those of them who had been taken by the Messiah craze. It had appealed very strongly to many men who were restrained from joining in the ghost dancing out of regard for myself and because they had given their promise to live as white men. But the religion, preached for his own sinister ends by Sitting Bull, was calculated to appeal to the Indian mind—and the Indian mind, as I have tried to show elsewhere, is attuned to a pitch altogether different to that of the white man. It is capable of great depths in some directions while childishly shallow, according to our standards, in others. These people had gone very close to a baptism of blood; they had seen destroyed in an instant the power of Sitting Bull; his medicine had proved altogether useless and ineffective, and their ideals were thus upset. So it was, that they came in to the agency and talked gravely and calmly enough of what had happened and speculated upon what was happening elsewhere. Those of their relatives and friends who had fled from the Reservation, scattered by the Sitting Bull affair, were few in number, comparatively, and they got no sympathy from those who were left. But they were excited under their cover of indifference and required careful handling—not that they had any notion of leaving the Reservation, but because the events that had transpired might adversely effect their attitude with regard to civilization.

With the guidance of affairs of the Reservation, the necessity for giving proper care to the families of the people killed, and the other conditions to which I have referred, it was a strenuous time at the Agency. Through it all the chiefs and influential men, chiefly, Gall, Grass, Gray Eagle, and other men of influence could be depended upon, and they exerted a most benign influence on the rest of the people, and I had little apprehension as to the future within the confines of the Reservation—if only the pernicious influence of the fault-finding busybodies and fakers outside did not have a baneful effect. All sorts of stories were spread through the press and many efforts were made to make it appear that I was not in sympathy with the military and that the War Department was not satisfied with my handling of the disaffected Indians. But the official reports of the military men and the comments of the superior officers put a quietus on all this.

There never was any disagreement between myself and the military men in the matter. I am proud of the fact that I had then, as I have now, many scores of excellent and cordial friends in the army and that I added to the number of them during that winter. I had been in thorough sympathy and touch with Colonel Drum all through the affair and there was not the slightest friction between the agency people and the soldiery at Fort Yates. This was a condition established during my residence as Agent at Standing Rock. The time had been when no civil word was passed between the civilians of the Agency and the military people of Fort Yates, during which time had a man on either side of the fence, dividing the Agency grounds from the Fort Yates Garrison limits, given any evidence of friendship for one on the other side, it was regarded sufficient to brand the friendly one as disloyal to his superior.

But all this had been changed and there was perfect accord on each side. Capt. E. G. Fechet, who commanded the Eighth Cavalry detachment supporting the Indian Police in the arrest of Sitting Bull, did full justice to the Indian Police in his report and this report was endorsed by Colonel Drum, and this brings me to another bit of official history in the form of a letter from Hon. John W. Noble, then secretary of the Interior, with some enclosures. Here is the letter:

DEPARTMENT OF THE INTERIOR
Washington, January 16, 1891.

James McLaughlin,
    U. S. Indian Agent, Standing Rock, N. D.
Sir:
    I enclose herewith a copy of the report of Captain E. G. Fechet, commanding Eighth Cavalry, Fort Yates, N. D., together with the report of Lieut. Col. W. F. Drum, commanding the post, to the Adjutant General, Department of Dakota, in relation to the arrest and death of Sitting Bull on the 15th Ult.
    In these reports, as well as in the endorsement of the General of the army forwarding them to the Secretary of War, special mention is made of your action as commendable and of that of the Indian Police as marked by bravery and fidelity in this affair to which your attention is particularly invited.
    Very respectfully,
        John W. Noble,
        Secretary.

This should dispose of the stories that were widely circulated at that time concerning the attitude of the army officers toward me as an Indian Agent, but I am moved to add some extracts from a letter written later that year by Capt. Jesse M. Lee, U. S. A., now Major General, retired, to Colonel Drum, and by the latter handed to me; I cherish it very highly as I had not the honor of Captain Lee's personal acquaintance until only a few months prior to this time. The Captain had a wide knowledge of the Indian affairs and knew the condition of things at many Agencies which he had visited officially. I quote from this letter, dated Chicago, August 20, 1891:

> I regret exceedingly that any man would think of making any complaints against Major McLaughlin, and I also regret that any credence should be given to such complaints against the best Indian Agent in the service. In my official reports through military channels I took pleasure in saying as much. I had heard much of Major McLaughlin's good work, but when I saw with my own eyes what he had done and was doing, I realized that the half had not been told me.
>
> The Department should hold up his hands and support him and his good wife in their grand work instead of permitting anyone to try to pull them down. If I had the opportunity of seeing Commissioner Morgan and talking to him, I would take especial delight in informing him fully as to my high opinion of Major McLaughlin as an Indian Agent and a gentleman.
>
> No greater wrong can be done to the Indian service, to the progress of the Indians, than to impair in any way the influence of such an agent as Major McLaughlin is well known to be. It is nothing less than an outrage. And adds that he fears that the high regard in which army officers hold Major McLaughlin may have something to do with the activity of the people who criticize him.

I may be pardoned for quoting this letter which is given as an indication of the general attitude of my friends of the army toward me in those days.

It was in the early and strenuous days of that winter that there floated into the Agency from the outside world a story that was at once funny and exasperating. Some string-fiend had sent out a fake to the effect that arrangements had been made, or were being made, for putting the remains of Sitting Bull on exhibition. When I heard of the story first, I paid no attention to it. I had been present at the burial of Sitting Bull, and I knew that his grave had not been disturbed. But, absurd as the story was, it attracted attention in the East and there are perhaps some people who still believe there may have been something in it. In any event, the fake was not permitted to get past without being officially noted, and I was not much astonished—considering the other absurd things that had been called officially to the attention of the Department—to receive one day an official communication concerning it.

At the time, Dr. T. A. Bland, an enthusiastic, if not always discreet, friend of the Indian, was at the head of the National Indian Defense Association. In that day the friends of the Indian in the East got much of their information as to the events in the camp of the people they would befriend from the public prints. The writers of Indian news generally got their information as to the Indian from imaginations that were not much exercised. But when the chief officer of the Indian Defense Association addressed a communication to the Indian Office it had to be given official attention. Dr. Bland heard, or read, that Sitting Bull was to be used for post mortem show purposes and he wrote the Commissioner of the Indian Affairs a letter which was referred to me for a report. Here is the letter:

NATIONAL INDIAN DEFENSE ASSOCIATION
Washington, D. C., December 27, 1890.
To the Honorable Commissioner,
    Indian Affairs, Washington, D. C.
Sir:

    I observe in the public press a statement to the effect that the body of Sitting Bull was removed from the coffin before it was buried and taken to a dissecting room. The reasonable supposition is that it is the intention of the parties having the matter in charge to make his bones a subject of speculation and perhaps his skin also, as the papers state that a Bismarck merchant offered $1,000 for it.

I beg to ask if you do not hold it the duty of the Government, as guardian of the Indians to inquire into this matter and take measures to punish any parties, whether Government officials or not, who may be found guilty of such desecration of the dead chief's body?

Respectfully,

T. A. Bland.

Looking back at it now it is all a ghastly joke, but at that time it was rather a serious matter in the aspect it presented to the public—this outcome of the fake of Bismarck string-fiend. Dr. Bland's letter was referred to me for an explanation, and without comment, by Commissioner Morgan, and as the body of Sitting Bull was never in my possession-except in that it was brought in from Grand River by the Indian police under my control—I could do nothing but refer the Bland letter to Colonel Drum with this endorsement:

Standing Rock Agency, January 23, 1891.

As the body of Sitting Bull was taken to the military post of Fort Yates upon its arrival from Grand River, this paper is respectfully referred to the commanding officer of Fort Yates for such information as he may be pleased to make concerning the matter to assist me in replying to the Commissioner's letter.

James McLaughlin,

U. S. Indian Agent.

Officially, Colonel Drum was not called upon to go into the matter. It was so absurd that he might have laughed at it and paid no attention to it whatever, but, courteously enough, he passed it on, referring it to the post surgeon for a brief statement of the facts in the case. The post surgeon made this report:

Post Hospital

Fort Yates, N. D., January 23, 1891.

Respectfully returned to the Post Adjutant.

I received the body of Sitting Bull about 4:30 P. M., on the 16th day of December, 1890, and it was in my custody until it was buried on the 17th. During that time it was not mutilated or disfigured in any manner. I saw the body sewed up in a canvas, put in a coffin and the lid screwed down and afterwards buried in the northwest corner of the post cemetery in a grave about eight feet deep, in the presence of Captain A. R. Chapin, assistant surgeon U. S. A., Lieut. P. G. Wood, 12th Infantry, Post Quartermaster, and myself.

H. M. Deeble,

A. A. Surgeon, U. S. A., Post Surgeon.

This was forwarded to me with this additional endorsement:

Fort Yates, N. D., January 24, 1891.

Respectfully returned to Indian Agent, James McLaughlin, inviting attention to third endorsement hereon. The grave does not appear to have been disturbed.

W. F. Drum,

Lieut. Col. Twelfth Infantry, Commanding Post.

From this it would appear that Sitting Bull was pretty effectually buried and that his body was intact. I returned to the Commissioner the reports with this last endorsement:

Fort Yates, N. D., January 27, 18910

Respectfully returned to the Honorable Commissioner of Indian Affairs inviting attention to the endorsements of the acting Assistant Surgeon and the Commanding Officer at Fort Yates.

The body of Sitting Bull, together with the dead policeman, was brought to the Agency in the afternoon of December 16th by the police (who were acting under the direction of the military) whence, after depositing the dead policeman, it (Sitting Bull's body) was taken at once

by the police, without removal from the wagon in which
it was brought from Grand River, to the post of Fort Yates
and left there in charge of the military authorities in pursuance of the Division Commander's orders to the Post
Commander before the arrest, directing the latter to secure the person of Sitting Bull. I saw Sitting Bull's remains
upon arrival at the Agency, and was present in the afternoon of December 17th, 1890, in the Military Cemetery
and saw his grave, which had been partly filled with soil
before I got there, and I feel confident that he was neither dissected nor scalped before burial and also quite
confident that his grave has not been disturbed since.

James McLaughlin,
U. S. Indian Agent.

That was the official end of Sitting Bull. I have no doubt that
his effigy decorated in such garb as would have forever discred-
ited the old medicine man among his followers, has been exhibited for the delectation of the gullible, but I am also very certain
that the grave beside which I stood last June, when I was moved to
write this story of the bloody end of the turbulent life of Sitting
Bull, contained all that death left of the once powerful prophet and
leader of the Sioux people.

MY FRIEND THE INDIAN
CHAPTER FIFTEEN
SHAVE HEAD'S CODE OF HONOR

The Story of a Man of the Hunkpapa Sioux
Who Fought Fiercely, Hated Thoroughly,
and Died for the White Man

Shave Head was of the Hunkpapas. There have been men of
his tribe who were better known to the white man. Sitting Bull,
whose medicine was not good for the white man, who lurked in the

background of all the evil that his people wrought for many a blood drenched year while the Sioux nation was putting up a merciless and dread protest against the usurpation of their hunting grounds by the white invader—Sitting Bull was also of the Hunkpapa. So, too, was Gall, man of brain and brawn, a "good Indian" ere he went to the spirit land and whose recognition of the mission of the white man to lead his people in the way of peace made largely for the good of those of us who lived on the Standing Rock Reservation. So was Crow King, Sitting Bull's lieutenant in the mad flight to Canada after the awful affair on the Little Big Horn, where Custer and his troopers died at the hands of the men of the Dakota nation. And so were Charging Eagle, Black Moon, Spotted Horn Bull, Circling Bear, Rain-in-the-Face—names with which Indians conjured in the days when braves painted for the warpath and the laurels of the field of blood were more regarded than the good will of the Reservation farmer who teaches the arts of peace that red men may live in the sweat of their brows.

All these and many more were of the house of the Hunkpapas and the names of the mispelled terror to the women of the frontier that was and is not, and the men who fought breast to breast with them for the right to live in peace in the land of the Dakotas. Theirs was the place of honor when the Sioux met in great council, theirs the guarded privilege of pitching their tents on the outer edge of the circle of bands, holding watch and ward at the gateway of the camp—and thence their name—Hunkpapa: "The Outer Edge."

And Shave Head was of the Hunkpapas. Disdaining the locks of the red people, his hard head was clipped in the fashion of the white man, yet no young man of his village taunted him because he wore no scalp lock, for he was quick in reprisal and none dared say that Shave Head's heart was soft in his dealings with a foe. As a hunter, and one whose word might be depended upon, he arrived at man's estate, and lived in peace until that day when Red Thunder, of the Yanktonais, crossed him at the beef issue.

In those days the hearts of the Sioux were not much inclined to the ways of the white man. The rations they took—when they hungered—and they listened to the promises of the white father, but they made no sign. And they liked the beef issue, for it was then permitted them to kill the beeves after their own fashion, one beast for every thirty souls, and the head man of each thirty divided the beef according to the right of might.

The Agency had but recently been moved to Standing Rock from the Grand River, and the beef issue took place on the east bank of the Missouri, where now sits the dying village of Winnona—the day of its prosperity faded into twilight with the passing of the Fort Yates Garrison. The turgid tide of the Missouri rolled its muddy flood between the Agency and the cattle corral, and the red men passed over to the north of Cat Tail Creek for the beef cattle they killed to their liking. And with them went Red Thunder, Bully and Bravo, with seven dead men waiting with the other ghosts for his spirit to pass over to the place of the shades and to point him out as a murderer of his kind. The old men turned their backs on Red Thunder and the young men passed him by or did his bidding, for his gun was ever ready and his knife within reach. In the fullness of his ruffian life was Red Thunder, and no man called him friend, even among his own people of the Lower Yanktonais.

Up and down the river the people covered the soft grass lands of the Missouri bottom. Men and women worked at the killing. Each head man of the thirty persons took his animal and rejoiced in the killing as he might have rejoiced in killing Pte, the buffalo. And Shave Head worked manfully at the cutting up of the beef that had fallen to his portion and joked with his friends as he made the division.

Into four quarters was the beef divided and the women rejoiced for the meat was fat and wholesome. "When Shave Head picks the beef, his eye is true and his choice makes our hearts glad," said an old woman and the people made their approval. Then a shadow fell on Shave Head and Red Thunder stood between him and the sun. The people, men, women, and children, fell away for Red Thunder was not good to look at. His hands and arms were smeared with blood, over his left shoulder was the double-barrelled shotgun that was inseparable from him since his last killing has put him at feud with the relatives of Yellow Eyes, who was found lying dead with his face in the pool he had been drinking from when the enemy shot him in the back. His blanket hung loosely from his shoulders and he dragged a quarter of beef with his right hand. Shave Head looked up, but said no word until Red Thunder, letting go of the quarter of beef he was dragging, seized one of those belonging to the party of thirty in which Shave Head shared. The youth, who was of fair proportions, arose immediately to his feet. The blanket that hung on his shoulders was his only garment except the breech cloth and his moccasins. As he arose, his hand closed over the Winchester that lay on the ground beside him.

"Why does Red Thunder lay his hands on my beef?" demanded Shave Head.

"Because Red Thunder sees that it is better than his own," sneered the brave.

"The beef is mine," said Shave Head.

"Red Thunder takes that which looks best to him," rejoined the other, and an evil look came over his face that made the women and children who had stood about Shave Head fall away from the pair standing over the beef.

"You must put down my beef," said Shave Head, and the people looked for the rash young man to fall dead when Red Thunder's weapon spoke. Since the first beef issue at Standing Rock Agency, Red Thunder had helped himself to the fattest and best quarter and no man had said him nay before. Thirty of the weaker ones might share a beef, but a quarter was Red Thunder's share and he was hated for a glutton as he was feared as a murderer.

"Why don't you take your beef," sneered the marauder.

"I will," said Shave Head, and the people turned their faces away that they might not see him die. The blanket slipped from Shave Head's shoulder and he bounded high in the air and backwards as the gun of Red Thunder fell naturally into the hollow of his arm, his finger on the trigger. Shave Head jumped about as one possessed and the women shrieked as the young man drew the fire of the evil-eyed killer. Twice the shotgun spoke; the range was point blank, but the spirits of the men he had murdered, as the Indians believed, turned away the weapon of Red Thunder. The stare of amazement he fixed on Shave Head as he saw him stand still unharmed, changed into the grin of death as the Winchester of Shave Head rang out and Red Thunder, the killer, pitched on his face. Shave Head walked up to his body and emptied the fifteen remaining shots into the prostrate form.

The thing was done, the slayer was slain, and no man could say that Shave Head might be blamed. But the code of the Dakota's did not permit that a man might be slain by arms and his relatives allow the slayer to go unscathed. Shave Head thought fast in that instant, and the thing he did saved him for a nobler death in a worthier cause. He filled the magazine of his gun, then before the Yanktonais, the brethren of Red Thunder, could act, he retreated to the top of a hill to the south and sitting there, taunted them.

"Red Thunder is dead," he shouted, "I killed him. Had he twenty lives I would take them all. Where is his brother or his cousin? Let them come and take the life of the slayer." Yet none offered him fight and they took the body of Red Thunder and built a scaffold near the mouth of Cat Tail Creek, close by the shores of the Missouri, and there they laid the killer, making provision for his dark journey. Pipes and tobacco and meat they placed by the body and white men and red men passing up and down the Missouri pointed to the lone body on the high place at the mouth of the Cat Tail and said, "Red Thunder is dead, and no one grieves."

And the heart of Shave Head was bad and bitter against the memory of the man who had caused him to become a slayer before the women and children, even though the deed was a deed of justice, and for many years when the people of the Agency heard that Shave Head had money, they listened for the speaking of a Winchester. For Shave Head kept alive the memory of his wrong and his deed of justice by buying a box of cartridges when he had the silver with which to purchase the same, going alone and quietly across the Missouri and firing sixteen shots through the remains of him that was Red Thunder—and this he did from time to time until scaffold and bones fell down to the earth and the ashes of Red Thunder mingled with the dust out of which the Great Spirit formed the man.

In the bitter gloom of a winter morning, Shave Head laid down his life for duty's sake. For weeks Sitting Bull had been making medicine that augered no good for the white people, which kept

him to his camp on the Grand River. Kicking Bear with his evange-
listic story of a journey to the end of the earth and an ascent to
heaven; the promise that had been given him that the earth would
be covered with a sea of mud that would engulf the white man and
leave the Indian free to roam the designated high places, teeming
with buffalo, had caught the fancy or fired the ambition of the old
chief. With his people he had been dancing the ghost dance for
many days and his band was ready to follow him to the place of the
coming of the Messiah, even though the trail followed the warpath.
And Sitting Bull and his camp on the Grand River was fast locked
in the sleep of exhaustion that followed days and nights of dancing and fasting.

Shave Head, steadfast in his likes and dislikes, had elected to
follow the white man. I, being then the Indian Agent, had sent to
Bull Head, who was the Lieutenant of Police, an order to arrest
Sitting Bull and bring him to the Agency. Shave Head was Bull
Head's first Sergeant and he knew no law but the word of the
father at the Agency and order of Bull Head.

Just about seven o'clock on the morning of December 15, 1890,
Bull Head, with Shave Head at his side and a group of Indian
policemen at his back, rode into the camp of Sitting Bull. The log
houses were dark, even the dogs made no sound. The officers of
the police entered the house of Sitting Bull and awakened him. The
old chief was told that he must go to the Agency. He acquiesced in
his arrest, but said he desired to dress in his best clothes, which
were in another cabin a few yards distant, and his younger wife
was sent to get the garments. This, together with his dressing, consumed about twenty minutes, giving his followers, who were all
camped near by, time to assemble and gather around the building.
Bull Head and his men led Sitting Bull out of the house into the
middle of the throng of Indians of Sitting Bull's band and when
they appeared outside, a menacing cry went up from the throats
of the ghost dancers and their eyes, red with the fatigue of the
frenzied dance, shot fire at Bull Head and Shave Head. In time of
action the men of the Sioux do not parley. Catch the Bear, one of
Sitting Bull's men, and upon Sitting Bull's order, raised his gun
and shot Bull Head through the body. The lieutenant of police fell,

and in falling, wheeled around and shot Sitting Bull in the left side. About the same instant, Strikes the Kettle, another of the ghost dancers, shot Shave Head, giving the Sergeant his death wound and his fighting was over; Bull Head, Shave Head, and Sitting Bull all falling together within a few feet of each other.

In that moment it was well for the whites and the red men of peace and the Indian police, that they had been drilled to the knowledge of swift attack.

After Bull Head and Shave Head had been wounded, command of the police detachment devolved upon Red Tomahawk, who signally distinguished himself that morning as narrated in Chapter XII.

The best of the fighting men of the Sioux were they and even while the smoke from Strikes the Kettle's gun still mingled with the steam of their breath, there was a fierce fusillade and when it was over, the men of Sitting Bull's band were running for the timber and five other policemen besides Shave Head and Bull Head lay on the ground, their blood an atonement for the deeds of their people. And eight of Sitting Bull's band would dance no more.

After being brought forty miles in an ambulance, First Sergeant Shave Head was still alive when he was carried into the Agency's Hospital; from a frightful wound in the pelvis, his vitals protruded and his hours were numbered. But his mind was clear and he forgot neither friend or foe. And his pain was forgotten when he saw the white men, doctors and Agency officials standing about his bedside and weeping, knowing that he would soon be dead. He beckoned to me to stoop over him.

"Did I do well, father," said Shave Head, and I could only nod, for the tightening in my throat choked me.

"Then I will die in the faith of the white men and to which my five children already belong, and be with them. Send for my wife, that we may be married by the Black Gown before I die."

And a white man was put on a swift horse and sent for the wife of Shave Head, 18 miles distant, that he might be married to her after the custom of the whites and die in peace. Shave Head had hitherto held to the faith of his fathers and, although he had given his children to the Black Gowns, he had all his life declined the invitation to become a member himself, for he was a man of strong heart and strong head, and no weakling to be moved by argument that he did not fully understand. But he saw that the days of the Indian and his tribal customs of marriage were over and he would wed according to the white man's rite the mother of his children and profess the white man's faith.

But death, riding a swifter steed than that given to the wife of Shave Head, came first to the side of the bed in the hospital. Day was breaking over the buttes east of the Missouri when Shave Head opened his eyes and asked if his wife had come and was told that she would arrive in a quarter of an hour.

"It will be too late," he said. Then to me, "Did I do my duty?" He was told that he had done well and that the whites would not forget him. "It is well," he said, and Shave Head turned his face to the wall and died.

Fifteen minutes later the wife of Shave Head wailed her lamentations at the door of the hospital and the whites, who owed much to her husband, solaced her. A granite shaft was erected at the head of Shave Head's grave to perpetuate the memory of this man who hated fiercely, loved well, and kept the faith to the death. And Shave Head's widow sits in her cabin on Standing Rock Reservation nursing the fragment of a hope that the Great Council of the whites will some day keep faith and give her a place on the pension rolls as the widow of a good soldier.

MY FRIEND THE INDIAN
CHAPTER FOURTEEN
HOW HAWKMAN RODE TO HIS DEATH

A Notable Achievement in Endurance
which Led an Indian Policeman to His Fate

On the Battle Roll of the Sioux Indian Police, Hawkman No. 2, is set down as David Hawkman; in the lodges of the Tetons he is still referred to as "Cetanwicasta," and somewhere in Washington there is pigeonholed a proposal to give his widow a pension. This last I mention casually and not in the hope of propitiating the pension giving powers, for Hawkman was only an Indian hero and they don't count for much in a time when heroes are made in the marts of trade. Hawkman was shot dead, the first man killed outright, in front of Sitting Bull's house at the time of the latter's arrest, and almost at the instant that the old chief fell. Hawkman had no business there. By all the laws of human nature he should have been sleeping the sleep of the just and the weary, in the consciousness of having performed a most tremendous feat in the accomplishment of a self-imposed duty. But fate, riding in the saddle with Hawkman, led him a mad chase over the trails of the Standing Rock Reservation to his doom. His ride upon that occasion is still talked of by the Standing Rock Sioux and, being naturally fatalists, often relate the ride to death that Hawkman made and just take it for granted that he should have been where he was when the bullet of a crazed ghost dancer found its billet in his breast.

Hawkman lived on the Grand River about four miles east of the camp of Sitting Bull. He had a family—a wife and four children. He was a working Indian and a good man. He had ambitions in the direction of a policeman's uniform and he had realized his ambition insofar that he had been made a special. During the ghost dancing I thought he had been brought under the influence of the prophets of the craze. He lived close enough to Sitting Bull to be easily reached and it is very certain that the Indians who lived in that neighborhood and rejected the domination of the chief and declined to admit the efficacy of his medicine was likely to have a bad time. It is no discredit to the memory of Hawkman for me to say that at that time—during the fall of 1890—I was not inclined to give him the confidence that I gave to Bull Head and Shave Head. The former who was First Lieutenant of the Indian Police had better judgment in the matter than I, and declared that Hawkman could be depended upon. It took some strength of mind for an untutored Indian to reject the ghost dancing religion and its promises, its assurance of an eternity of those good things which most appeal to a savage. And it required moral and physical courage to remain in the same neighborhood with Sitting Bull and yet stand out against him. Therefore, I did not lay it against Hawkman when I heard that he was inclined to give ear to the false prophets. But I did not let him have any part in the surveillance of Sitting Bull, which was under the direction of Lieutenant Bull Head. As a matter of fact, very few of the people—I might say only a couple of those who could be depended upon under any circumstances—knew any of the details of the plan that had been framed to prevent the chief from folding his tents and silently fleeing in the night. Therefore, it came about that Hawkman's part in the affair on the Grand River was entirely casual, so far as human knowledge could go.

The Standing Rock Reservation was then a country of magnificent distances. It is eighty-three miles from the agency to the western boundary of the Reservation, and while none of the Indians had permanent camps at or near the westernmost boundary, there were a considerable number who lived more than fifty miles from the Agency. We knew of many who practically spent all their time on the trail between the Agency and their homes coming after their bi-weekly rations. And they would dawdle along the trail with travois or wagons and take a week or nearly a week to come in, then, getting their rations, they would remain around and visit and start home only to arrive there in time to start back from the next beef issue. They could travel with plenty of speed when they wanted to, but it was notorious that a good many of them managed to lead a nomadic life, confined to the boundaries of the Reservation. In the winter this was a fearful trip, and the sufferings of those who got through storms with their lives pointed the necessity for putting up some sort of shelter for the travelers—a shelter that would permit them to rest in comfort at least one night on the journey. With this object in view, I had made arrangements to put up a station, consisting of a house for wayfarers and shelter for the teams—enough to shed a dozen or so ponies—on Oak Creek, twenty-two miles from the Agency and eighteen miles from Sitting Bull's camp on the Grand River. The logs for this station were being brought out that fall of the Ghost Dancing and this fact was of assistance in deluding Sitting Bull and his people into a sense of security when a detail of police was sent to the station, ostensibly to work on the structure, actually to be within reach when the order was given for the arrest of the medicine man. Hawkman No. 2 was engaged in bringing logs up from the Grand River for the buildings.

He left his home some time during the day of December 13th with a team of oxen drawing a load of logs. He got to Oak Creek rather late in the day and remained there over night. For some reason that was never ascertained he got up very early in the morning of the 14th, hitched up his cattle and started for home. He must have had a very early start, for he was at Grand River, near his own place, about ten o'clock A. M. Upon his arrival at Grand River he was met by Lieutenant Bull Head and told that he was detailed to carry a message to the Agent at Standing Rock. The message was that written by day school teacher, J. M. Carignan, at the suggestion of Bull Head, notifying me that Sitting Bull was preparing to leave the Reservation. Hawkman did not know the nature of the message but was proud of the distinction that the service would give him, doubtless thinking that it would bring nearer to him the coveted honor of the blue uniform and a place on the permanent police roll. He mounted his horse, which was an exceptionally good one, and put the animal through a pace that scorched the ground behind him for the forty miles distance. He was nearly exhausted when he arrived at the Agency, and I sent him to the police quarters giving instructions that he be taken care of and kept there all night. He was very anxious to be doing something, but I was not thinking of sending him back to the river. Moreover I wanted to send Sergt. Red Tomahawk, whom I was certain could be trusted to carry through the important orders that were going to Lieutenant Bull Head and who was intelligent enough to properly convey the verbal directions.

Hawkman was received at the police quarters with due honor as the bearer of important tidings, though what news he brought remained a problem to the Indians, no man knowing, except those concerned, that orders had been given for the arrest of Sitting Bull.

A good supper was prepared for the courier, but he ate little and talked less. He had the air of a man who was impressed by something that impended, but he knew nothing of the cause of his uneasiness and depression. It was observed by the policeman on duty at their headquarters that he could not rest. There being an air of expectancy about the Agency at the time, no particular attention was paid to Hawkman when, impelled by fate, he went out and got his horse that he had ridden from Grand River, forty miles that day, and mounted and started back on the trail that led him home and then on. He got home during the night, but could not remain there. He got another mount and rode to Bull Head's house, which he found deserted by the police. They had gone on to Gray Eagle's—whose two sisters were married to Sitting Bull, and were presently to be reduced to widowhood. There he found the policemen had started for the camp of Sitting Bull, and full of the inspiration that was leading him on to his death, he followed the trail and caught up with Bull Head's command as the detachment was entering the Sitting Bull camp.

Hawkman rode with the detachment into the camp and, while Sitting Bull was making ready for the journey, he sat in his saddle with the other policemen waiting for the prisoner to be brought out of the house. He was not affected by the flashing eyes and glowering faces of the ghost dancers, who gathered about with rifles in their hands and threatened the police, and no suggestion of fear stirred him when Sitting Bull came forth and began railing, but he brought his Winchester to a ready when Sitting Bull called upon his people to rescue him, and in that moment he died: There were four shots fired in rapid succession, mortally wounding Bull Head and Shave Head, and killing Sitting Bull, and at the fifth shot Hawkman fell dead. He had ridden not less—rather more—than 120 miles in 22 hours (18 miles of it by ox team) and was in at the death.

I am reminded to state here that my orders for the arrest of Sitting Bull were not carried out to the letter, my verbal instructions to Lieutenant Bull Head being that he take a spring wagon with him when he went to make the arrest so that he might place Sitting Bull in it and leave the camp at once, but in the excitement of the moment the wagon was forgotten. Had a wagon been taken to the camp there might not have been any bloodshed, for it was while waiting for Sitting Bull to change his clothes and have his horse brought from the corral that his followers gathered in front of the house, and were it not for the delay thus occasioned, might have been gotten into a wagon and hurriedly taken away without any bloodshed. As it was, when a wagon was obtained for the purpose of bringing in the bodies of the dead policeman and that of Sitting Bull, there was something like a disagreement, or, as near it as discipline would permit. Sergt. Red Tomahawk, who succeeded to the command of the police after Bull Head had been wounded, had the Lieutenant's instructions to take Sitting Bull into the Agency and it was not his concern that he could not take him in alive. Sitting Bull was dead, but that did not change the letter of the Sergeant's instructions, so he ordered that the body be put into the wagon with the remains of the four Indian policemen who had been killed in the fight. The members of his force demurred, for was he not responsible for the death of their comrades? They objected to having him put in the same wagon with their friends, but Red Tomahawk was obdurate, and insisted upon carrying out Lieutenant Bull Head's order. Finally there was a compromise by the policemen agreeing that Sitting Bull might be taken in with the bodies of the others, provided that he be put in the bottom of the wagon, which was done, with the other bodies being put on the top of him and the ghastly load was brought into the Agency thus, with all that was earthly of Sitting Bull regarded as slightly as though he had never arrogantly taken the first place in following that same trail when he was living.

Speaking of the dead reminds me that out of the death of the hostiles who fell with Sitting Bull, there sprang the foundation of a Christian mission in that settlement on the Grand River. The Indians killed had been allowed to lie unburied. The policemen had no time to bury them and if they had, it is to be doubted that they would have taken the trouble, for, although they were excellent policemen and good soldiers, they were still Indians, and it was no part of their creed to bury the dead of the enemy. Soon after the fight, the Rev. Thomas L. Riggs, a missionary and son of the famous missionary to the Sioux, arrived on the ground. The camp was deserted, the men who survived the fight having betaken themselves out of the way to the south.

Mr. Riggs, after the fashion of the frontier missionary who does that thing which he finds to his hand, assisted by a few Indians who accompanied him, performed the Christian duty of burying the dead. He made a common grave for the seven ghost dancers and put them away decently. There was practically no Christianity in the camp before that day, but the Indians, when they returned, were so impressed by the charitable act, and the further fact that their friends and relatives had been buried by this particular minister of a particular church—the Congregational—that they embraced the faith offered them by him and a very considerable mission was established—all going to show that works, as well as faith, appeal strongly to the red man from a missionary point of view.

Coachwhip Publications

CoachwhipBooks.com

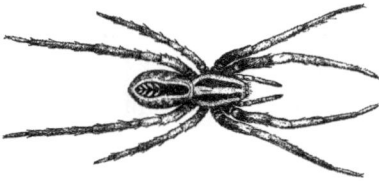

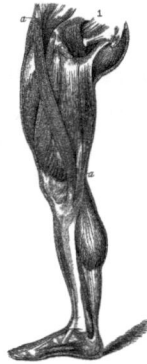

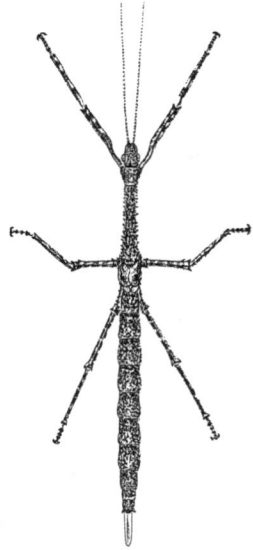

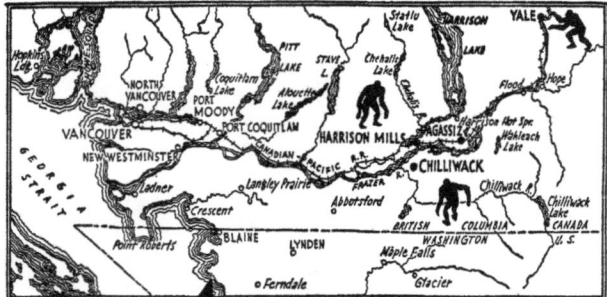

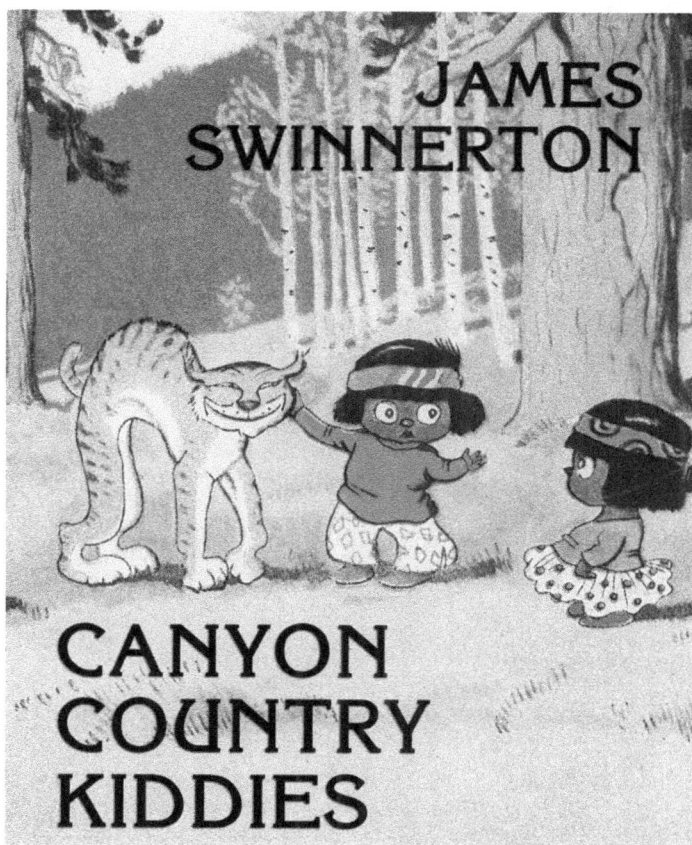

CANYON COUNTRY KIDDIES

JAMES SWINNERTON

ISBN 1-61646-070-9

BioFortean Reprint

Sculptured Anthropoid Ape Heads Found In or Near the Valley of the John Day River, a Tributary of the Columbia River, Oregon

James Terry

SCULPTURED ANTHROPOID APE HEADS

ISBN 1-61646-069-5

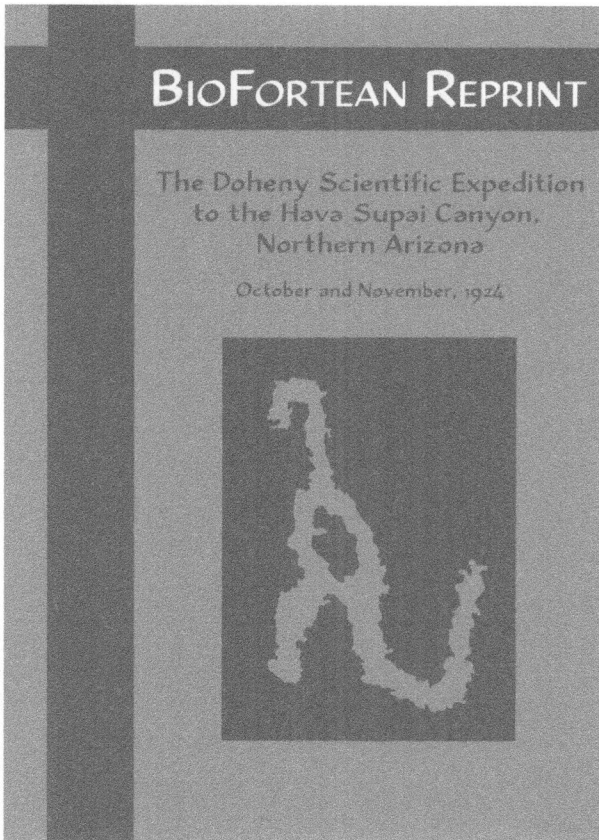

BioFortean Reprint

The Doheny Scientific Expedition to the Hava Supai Canyon, Northern Arizona

October and November, 1924

HAVA SUPAI PETROGLYPHS

ISBN 1-61646-068-7

www.ingramcontent.com/pod-product-compliance
Lightning Source LLC
Chambersburg PA
CBHW022334280326
41934CB00006B/630